SUSAN B. ANTHONY
And Justice For All

Jeanne Gehret

Verbal Images Press

Fairport, New York

Copyright © 1994 by Jeanne Gehret
Cover and inside llustrations copyright © 1994 by Verbal Images Press
Printed in The United States of America

Publisher's Cataloging in Publication

Gehret, Jeanne, 1953-
  Susan B. Anthony and justice for all / by Jeanne Gehret;
  illustrated by Jeff Lennox.
  128 p. 22 cm. illus.
  Includes index, chronology, and glossary
  Summary: Biography of the New York State feminist who
  advocated women's suffrage, abolition of slavery, and
  temperance.

  ISBN 0-9625136-9-5 (cloth)
  ISBN 0-9625136-8-7 (pbk.)

  1. Anthony, Susan B. (Susan Brownell), 1820-1906—
Juvenile Literature. 2. Feminists—United States—Biography—
Juvenile Literature. 3. Suffragettes—United States—Biogra-
phy—Juvenile Literature. [1. Anthony, Susan B. (Susan
Brownell), 1820-1906 2. Feminists—United States—Biography.
3. Suffragettes—United States—Biography.]
I. Title. II. Lennox, Jeff, illus.

HQ1414.A55G2593 1994 324.6'23'0924 [B]

Verbal Images Press
19 Fox Hill Drive • Fairport, New York 14450
(716) 377-3807 • Fax (716) 377-5401

Acknowledgments

For historical consultation:
Mary Huth and Lorie Barnum, The Susan B.
Anthony Memorial, Rochester, New York;
MaryEllen Snyder,Women's Rights National
Historical Park, New York

For consultation in multicultural studies:
Rene Montenegro, Director of Multicultural
Student Affairs, Skidmore College

For editing:
Jennifer Spungin
Cary Hull
Geri Seigneur

Table of Contents

Preface

Susan B. Anthony led an exciting life and did many great things. Working against injustice wherever she saw it, she crisscrossed North America many times. She broke unfair laws in her effort to change them; "kidnapped" a woman away from a cruel husband; faced angry mobs; and gathered 400,000 signatures asking Congress to outlaw slavery. So impressed were the lawmakers that they did as she asked.

She was a person of immense energy, kindness, and daring who lived long enough to write her own history (or perhaps we should say *herstory*).

Susan worked 50 years to achieve equal rights for women, but she never saw this goal accomplished during her lifetime. However, 14 years after her death, when Congress finally passed a law allowing women to vote, they named it after her.

Susan began as a simple Quaker girl and, throughout her 86 years, worked very hard for every penny she earned. From her earliest days, her riches lay in the companionship of family and friends who believed that one person can make a difference. Even in her rather ordinary childhood there were hints of the great woman she would become.

Susan B. Anthony, in 1868, posed with her face turned,
probably to disguise her weak eye.
University of Rochester

Chapter One: 1820-1838
Why Can't a Woman...?

Susan B. Anthony paced back and forth past the window overlooking the street. It was the spring of 1838, and she was looking forward to going home from boarding school. After what seemed like hours, she saw what she was waiting for, and flung open the front door. Guelma, Susan's older sister, followed close behind.

Grabbing her skirts and petticoats in both hands, 18-year-old Susan rushed to the gate of Miss Moulson's school for girls. For once she ignored her teacher's icy reminders that young ladies should walk instead of run.

Father stretched and climbed down from the carriage. Using the special speech of the Quakers, he teased his daughters, "Have thee been waiting, girls?"

"Only since dawn," Guelma, 20, joked back with a twinkle in her eye. Members of this tight-knit religious group dressed simply and said 'thee' and 'thou' instead of 'you' and 'your'.

Susan hoisted her bags up to the carriage and jumped in to sit beside her father and sister. Then the two girls quickly asked their father for details of every family member. Hannah, 17, was thinking of being a teacher, Father replied. Daniel, 14, had recently carved a whistle out of wood. Their shy 11-year-old sister Mary could hardly wait for Susan to walk through the door. Four-year-old Merritt was following his older brother everywhere these days. And for this homecoming, Mother had baked the special bread that Susan especially liked.

§§§

Bumping along in the carriage, Susan began savoring memories of the family she had been longing to see. She thought back on the courtship stories of her parents when they were young. Her mother, Lucy Read Anthony, had been raised a Baptist and enjoyed singing, dancing, and pretty clothes. In fact, when Father fell in love with her, Mother had been the most popular girl in the neighborhood! Mother loved Father so much that when she married him, she put away most of her lighthearted ways out of respect for his plain Quaker customs. However, she never joined the church herself, feeling she could not live up to its high standards.

Susan was born in Adams, Massachusetts in 1820 when her sister Guelma was two years old. Soon little Hannah was born, and the three sisters loved each other very much. When Susan was four, Mother became pregnant with Susan's brother Daniel. Shortly before the birth, Mother sent the three girls to Grandmother Read's for six weeks. Grandmother and Grandfather taught Susan to read, and the little girl so delighted in her new ability that she practiced for long hours every day. But when the daughters returned home, Mother was horrified to discover that young

Susan's left eye was crossing — apparently from eyestrain.

She urged Susan to stop reading so that her eyes could relax and return to normal, but every once in awhile they still looked crossed. For this reason, Susan often felt self-conscious about her appearance. When she got older and had her picture taken, she usually turned her crossed eye away from the camera. In other pictures she wore glasses (which she did not truly need) to disguise that eye.

In 1826, when Susan was six years old, the Anthonys moved to Battenville in western New York. As Father built his business there, the tiny village grew, too. By 1836 it had expanded from just a few houses to a thriving town with two churches, a store, a post office, a cotton factory, two mills, a tavern, and about forty homes, many of which he had built for his employees. Two miles further down the Battenkill River, he owned more factories and mills in Hardscrabble, a village as ugly as its name. The business became so successful that Father was able to build his family a brand new, 14-room home with all the modern comforts, including four fireplaces.

Father often made unusual choices and got away with it. Almost everyone, including many Quaker elders and preachers, drank liquor at all hours of the day and night. Father, however, disapproved of such drinking, so he refused to serve alcohol to the men who came to help build houses for workers. Father's business partner warned, "The men will not come to the 'raising' unless they can have their gin."

"Then the houses will not be raised," Father replied

calmly, and sent out invitations anyway. On house-raising day, Mother served lots of lemonade, gingerbread, donuts, and coffee, and no one seemed to miss the liquor. Best of all, not a single accident marred the project, and everyone went home sober.

Sitting in the carriage on her long ride home, Susan recalled Sally Ann, one of Father's workers that she had grown to admire. The year Susan was twelve, another millworker fell sick for two weeks and Father let Susan do that woman's job for full pay. Several times during those weeks the boss, Elijah, had called for Sally Ann to untangle the threads when they became caught in the machinery.

Susan asked her father why he didn't make Sally Ann the overseer. After all, the young woman seemed to know more about weaving than Elijah.

But Father replied firmly, "It would never do to have a woman overseer in the mill."

Susan loved her father deeply. Sometimes, however, the way he treated women just didn't make sense to her. Still, his opinions on education, women, and drinking had a lasting effect on her life.

As a Quaker, Father often repeated teachings given by his sister, who preached at the Sunday Meeting. Like others in his church, Father believed that both girls and boys should receive a good education. Because she grew up in both a family and a church circle where women's minds were valued, Susan naturally assumed that such equality was normal. So when the town schoolmaster refused to teach Susan long division as a child, she ran home and protested this injustice to her father. Soon he started a school right in his own home. During the evenings, he offered classes to all of his millworkers — both women and men.

Most of the Quakers Susan knew ignored society's silly rules about women. They even called themselves "Friends" to everyone. Susan could not understand, then, why Father would encourage women to become smarter workers, but later ignore their skills and give the good jobs to men. Like other business owners, he paid his female employees half a man's wage. Susan thought this was unfair.

After awhile she realized that the neighbors were equally puzzled by her father's views on women, but for a different reason. They thought that he was wasting his time, effort, and money on them. Like the schoolmaster, they could see no reason to teach girls much more than household duties. After all, wouldn't a woman always have a father or husband to take care of her? If so, then why did Father encourage all of his seven children to support themselves?

The neighbors shook their heads when Susan and her sisters spent summers of their teenage years teaching school. Why did Father allow his daughters to work when he was such a wealthy man? The girls should be home helping their mother Lucy, neighbors said.

Susan wondered why her father did not hire servants. He could certainly afford them, and poor Mother could use an extra pair of hands. So although it was endless drudgery, Susan did all she could to help with hauling water, spinning, weaving, sewing, washing, ironing, and preserving food for the family of eight. At times the busy household grew to include even more people, such as the workers who built their new home. Of course, when Grandmother and Grandfather Read grew very old, Mother took them under her own roof and nursed them. Sometimes Mother herself became ill with the endless hard work.

When Grandmother and Grandfather Read died, they wanted to give Mother $10,000, which was a lot of money in those days. But Father's business had begun to fail, and he knew that if they accepted the money, they would have to use it to pay his debts. So Mother's brother Joshua agreed to keep the money for the Anthonys until all their debts were paid.

§§§

Now Susan was going home to be with her family. When Miss Moulson's girls' school was several miles behind, Father gently brought Susan back to the present with disturbing news. Susan and Guelma would not be returning to that school, he said. Like mist, the girls' holiday mood vanished as they heard the terrible news: Father had lost everything in the depression that gripped the United States that year. He could no longer afford to keep the mills, the houses he had built for his workers, the store, or even their home and household goods.

How long until they had to sell? Susan wanted to know, her blue eyes a sea of concern. Father replied that they would have to start packing the house soon. All of the Anthonys' belongings would be sold at an auction next month.

Over the next few days they covered 300 miles from the school in Philadelphia to their home in eastern New York State. Everywhere they saw signs of the depression, which had begun when a change in the nation's banking system made money scarce. Factories and stores had closed, Father reported, and people had no work.

As Father steered the horses around the last corner of the street to the Anthony home, Susan viewed the house with a mixture of delight and sorrow. While at school she had written many homesick letters about her longing to be in the familiar place with those she loved. But now that she was here, the fine house, barn, and factories would have to be sold and Father would have to start over again. How would everyone in the family survive if Father couldn't earn any money?

§§§

Susan never forgot how difficult it was to pack the items the family would sell to pay Father's debts. The big house with the polished floors and light green woodwork had always been orderly. She hated to take things apart and make a mess. Besides, getting everything ready for the auction was so hard on Mother.

One day while they were packing, Mother pulled a pile of embroidered pillowcases from the wide dresser drawer and asked Mary to count them. Susan interrupted, "Oh, Mother, do we have to sell those? They were a wedding present from your mother, weren't they?"

Mother nodded sadly. "Yes, but everything must go on the list to be sold."

"Even our pocketknives?" called Daniel sadly from

the room that he shared with his brother Merritt.

"Even the flour, coffee, tea, and sugar? And the silver spoons from Grandmother Read?" said Hannah, coming upstairs from the kitchen.

"Everything — even your underclothes," Mother replied firmly.

Hannah wanted to know why they had to put Mother's spoons into the auction. After all, those spoons had belonged to her long before she ever met Father. They didn't have anything to do with his business debts, did they?

Yes, they did, Mother explained. When she married their father, everything she owned became his property. Under the law, the husband owned everything — he could even keep money that the wife earned and send the young children out to work against her wishes. Of course, their father would never do that, she assured her children hastily.

Susan listened in silence. She had heard of fathers who became drunk and gambled away all the family's money, leaving the wife and children to fend for themselves. Such a fate was too horrible to think about. At least her mother had been spared this embarrassment, she thought gratefully.

Mary finally voiced the question that everyone had been wanting to ask. How would they live without food and clothing?

Uncle Joshua had offered to buy the things they needed most, Mother reassured her children. He would let the Anthonys use them and pay him back as soon as they could.

Chapter Two: 1838-1845

Earning Her Own Way

Careworn from packing, Mother sat down to a simple family dinner. As soon as grace was said, Guelma and Susan revealed the plans they had been discussing so eagerly all afternoon. Now that they had gotten higher education at Miss Moulson's, they could teach full-time. They would be self-sufficient, just as Father always wanted. And they could send the money home to help the family.

Mother and Father exchanged glances. The girls' offer hung in the silence for several moments before Father nodded gratefully. But, he added, he wanted to keep track of every penny and pay the money back as soon as he could.

As it turned out, Guelma and Hannah married and moved away from the family within a few years, leaving Susan as the only grown, unmarried daughter to send wages home.

Soon after that, Susan started her 14-year teaching career. Much later, she realized just how wise her parents had been in their insistence on their daughters' getting enough education to earn their own way. When the Anthonys suddenly became poor, Susan was ready to support herself. She continued to do so for the rest of her long life. Because she gave so much of her time and money to the cause of women's rights, she never became wealthy. However, this never bothered her, because by keeping to the simple Quaker life-style she learned as a child, she always had what she needed.

After moving from Battenville, Father tried to establish a lumber business in Hardscrabble, New York, but with money so scarce, no one could afford wood to erect new buildings. Saddened, the Anthonys packed up again and moved in 1845 — this time more than 100 miles west to Rochester, New York.

A Quaker aunt warned Mother that Rochester was known for the hard-drinking men who rode the packet boats up and down the Erie Canal. The daughters and sons of such men ran the streets in rags, with nothing to eat.

But Mother replied that there was a large Quaker group in Rochester, and they had already offered to introduce the Anthonys to other Friends. Besides, she said, the farm they had bought wasn't anywhere near the canal.

Mother used her inheritance from her parents to make the first payment on the farm. Three years later, New York State changed the law to say that women could own property, and the deed was registered in her name.

Mother and the Anthony daughters had done a lot to keep the Anthonys out of the poorhouse, and Father appreciated it. Years later, when Susan needed to borrow money for the woman's cause, he lent it gladly.

Chapter Three: 1846-1850
Seeking a Different Path

From 1846 to 1849, Susan lived with her married cousin Margaret while working as headmistress of the girls' department at the school in Canajoharie, about 180 miles east of Rochester. There she won praise for her teaching from the townspeople as well as the attentions of many men. She had many dates, but after awhile she lost interest in them because the men so frequently became drunk at social gatherings. Like her father, she despised drinking.

Margaret and her husband Joseph did not follow Quaker ways. Little by little, they encouraged Susan to buy a fancy purse, wear colorful plaid dresses, and even go to dances, which were strictly forbidden among Friends. Susan missed her two married sisters, who hardly ever responded to her letters anymore. Thus, she took Margaret to her heart as her closest friend and relative.

Susan also joined the Daughters of Temperance, a group of women who spoke strongly about the evils of drinking alcohol. They emphasized that many fathers and husbands spent the family money on liquor, depriving women and children of food and clothing. They also pointed out that alcoholism often led to drunkenness and violence. Stronger liquor laws would solve many problems, they believed.

One evening, when this group had a dinner, Susan gave a speech challenging women to talk in public about liquor. The next morning word spread all over town that the teacher was the smartest woman in Canajoharie.

While Susan was living in Canajoharie, Margaret became very ill during pregnancy; Susan helped her through the long and difficult birth. "I never slept a wink," Susan wrote her mother. "I went to school the next morning, and every time one of the girls would speak, I imagined it was Margaret's groan."

After the baby was born, Margaret grew weaker. Susan devoted herself to nursing her cousin and taking over the care of the entire household while Joseph hardly lifted a finger. Since she was considered an "old maid" living under Joseph's roof, he felt that she owed him these efforts. This bothered her so much that she wrote to her brother, "No one feels that it is anything out of the common course of things for me to sacrifice my every feeling...to gratify those with whom I mingle." When Margaret died, Susan felt she had lost her only friend.

That same year Susan learned that a new headmaster was going to lead the Canajoharie school; she did not like this man or want to work with him. After Margaret's death, Susan longed to be near her family who loved and appreciated her, so she moved back to the farm in Rochester. Her father had taken a job selling insurance in Syracuse, and suggested that Susan manage the planting, harvesting, and selling of crops. Glad to leave Canajoharie, she agreed.

Back on the farm in Rochester, Susan found many opportunities to continue her temperance activities. Whenever she got a chance, she traveled to neighboring cities and towns to hear speeches about doing away with alcohol; she also raised money for the cause. Such reform movements, which aimed to improve society by doing away with a particular problem, kept people very busy during the 1800s. In those days before television and daily newspapers, people often gathered in town and church halls to hear traveling experts talk about politics, slavery, religion, and temperance. Town folk welcomed such meetings as a chance to talk to their neighbors and catch up on the news in the world beyond. This was especially true in upstate New York, where farming communities had very little to do during the long, snowy winters.

In that time, however, most of the speakers were men because women were so busy with housework that they had little energy to discuss matters beyond their homes. Unlike Susan, very few women had learned much beyond basic reading and writing in school. What good was it to think about reforming society when right in their own households were so many floors to sweep, socks to mend, babies to feed, and shirts to iron? Even when women did attend a public speech, they were expected to keep quiet, listen, and learn.

The brave women who had dared to act differently were sharply criticized. Back in 1837, Angelina Grimke boldly stood up in public to speak against slavery in New York City. Her listeners became so upset that they burned down the building. In 1848, Elizabeth Blackwell became the first woman in the world to graduate from medical school. That same summer, Elizabeth Cady Stanton organized the first Woman's Rights Convention in Seneca Falls, New York. At the meeting Mrs. Stanton said that women should work in any job they liked (even preaching), keep the wages they earned, divorce husbands who used all the family money to buy liquor, and even vote.

Susan had to miss this convention because it took place while she was still teaching in Canajoharie. When it met again in Rochester a few weeks later, her father, mother, and sister Mary attended and gave her an enthusiastic report. Although some of these new ideas sounded right to Susan, she was not yet convinced that women needed to vote. She said to her father, "I think you are getting ahead of your times."

However, she would have enjoyed hearing more from those lively women about temperance. Having worked for temperance for several years by now, Susan longed to support herself as a traveling lecturer on this issue. But how could she, when women were not even supposed to speak in public? Feeling that this choice was not open to her, for two years she threw herself into the farming life.

On weekends Father came home and a large group of Quakers gathered around him to discuss another reform movement called antislavery. Believing that God had created all people equal — whether Black or White, male or female — the Friends considered it deeply wrong that White people should force Black people to work for them.

Frederick Douglass, ex-slave, lived near Susan B. Anthony
in Rochester, New York. Susan worked with him and
many others to abolish slavery.
University of Rochester

Susan B. Anthony And Justice For All

One Sunday, the antislavery discussion in the parlor reached a peak. Susan took a breath, ready to offer her opinion. Just then, a forgotten pot boiled over on the stove, and she hurried back to the kitchen. She sighed. Must she always feel so torn between her desire to cook well and join the conversation?

It was now 1849, and 29-year-old Susan was becoming weary of this conflict between her regular duties and her wide-ranging interest in reform.

As she stirred the soup, she strained to hear the talk in the other room. Frederick Douglass, who had been a slave himself, said that abolition would not go far enough to right the wrongs against African-Americans in the United States.

It's not enough to just do away with slavery, the Black man argued. Black people also need the right to vote and elect the country's lawmakers.

The Quaker woman at his side shook her head vigorously. Slaves would never get the vote! Did anyone really think that White men, who were the only ones allowed to vote, would change the law to say slaves could vote, too? No, she asserted, White men would just as soon give the vote to women as to Blacks!

Joining the discussion at last, Susan asked Mr. Douglass if he had received many parcels that week. She spoke in the code of the Underground Railroad, a series of safe havens for runaway slaves as they journeyed to freedom in Canada, where slavery was against the law. The Douglass home in Rochester was only about ten miles from Lake Ontario, which bordered Canada, so it was almost the last stop.

The slaves, or "parcels," as they were called, did

not really have the advantage of riding on trains. They were too poor to buy a ticket, and no White master would ever pay for his slave to escape! Instead, they had to walk most of the way. Usually they traveled at night so they would not be seen. At Douglass' "station," Rochester folks fed and clothed the runaway slaves for the rest of their journey toward freedom in Canada.

Turning to Susan, Douglass replied that eleven people jammed his station that day, and one was a little boy in rags. Mother quickly offered to take over some of Merritt's outgrown breeches and shirts.

Douglass asked Susan if she would add some ointments to Mother's package, and some of her famous cream biscuits.

Susan nodded eagerly. She would also add a jar of the raspberry preserves she had made and some of the green beans she had picked on the farm. After so many years of teaching, she felt relieved to be doing something to right the wrong of slavery. Of course, she longed to do more than cook for the cause. But for now, that was all she could do.

As Susan put away her mother's dishes that evening, she wondered if she would ever have her own household to manage. Within the last two years she had turned down two marriage proposals because she did not love the men and because she did not want to be a traditional wife like her mother. But how could an unmarried woman afford to live? During the last 13 years, she had made quite a success of teaching, often taking over a school where a male teacher had failed. Yet she still earned only one dollar for every four that a man earned. She wondered if she could ever make enough money to support herself that way.

Even while her hands were busy with household tasks, Susan's active mind constantly ranged beyond the tasks on the farm. By the winter of 1850, she was attending so many temperance and antislavery meetings that her sister Mary teased, "When you get a husband and children, I hope you will treat them better than you did your raspberry plants, and not leave them to their fate at the beginning of winter."

The Sunday antislavery discussions satisfied a deep desire in Susan's soul. However, it was a long time between Sundays. Susan longed to fill all seven days a week with such worthwhile concerns. She asked herself, "What service can I render humanity; what can I do to help right the wrongs of society?"

Chapter Four: 1851
Opposites Attract

Seneca Falls, New York looked like just another sleepy town to the average person. To Susan, however, it meant home to one of the most exciting female minds in the country — Elizabeth Cady Stanton.

Unlike Susan, Mrs. Stanton was married with several children. She had traveled to Europe and knew famous antislavery workers that Susan respected.

The daughter of a wealthy judge, Mrs. Stanton (as Susan always called her friend) had studied Latin and Greek like a man and spent many hours poring over her father's law books. No wonder she wrote and spoke with such imagination and power. She had convinced Frederick Douglass and many of Susan's other friends that women had no more freedom than Black slaves.

Susan wanted to meet this remarkable woman.

Her chance to do so finally came in the spring of 1851 when Susan, now 31, visited a friend in Seneca Falls. To Susan's disappointment, however, Mrs. Stanton said hello briefly and then hurried away, saying that she had to get home before her two lively sons tore the house apart. A few days later, they met

Elizabeth Cady Stanton posed in 1848
with her two sons, Daniel and Henry.
Library of Congress

again. Susan was glad that this time they had a longer chance to talk.

As they got to know each other better, Mrs. Stanton told Susan how she had gone to England with her husband to an abolitionist meeting in 1840. She and the Quaker abolitionist Lucretia Mott had been invited to attend the World Antislavery Convention as representatives from the United States, but they were not allowed to speak at the meeting because they were women. Worse yet, they were made to sit behind a curtain while the men talked! Invisible and silent, they followed the men's speeches the best they could and carried on lively discussions among themselves.

Mrs. Stanton felt as restless about motherhood and domestic duties as Susan felt about teaching and farming. In many other ways, however, the two friends were opposites. Mrs. Stanton never lived in poverty or had to work to support her family, as Susan did. Mrs. Stanton had enjoyed good teachers who taught her style and confidence in her writing and speaking.

But Susan, under Miss Moulson's fussy and harsh instruction, had grown to dread writing anything except diaries or letters. "Whenever I take a pen in hand I seem to be mounted on stilts," she lamented. Mrs. Stanton, who eventually gave birth to seven children, was short and rounded, with pretty curls; Susan, childless, was tall and thin and quite plain.

Despite their differences, these two women shared a dedication to the cause that bonded them together. Moreover, the friendship with this remarkable woman was exactly what Susan needed to get her going. Even though Mrs. Stanton had no trouble putting thoughts into words, her family responsibilities kept her home most of the time. Susan used the freedom of her unmarried life to carry information to Seneca Falls and manage the children while her friend wrote. Then Susan spread Mrs. Stanton's ringing phrases about woman's rights to faraway places.

Susan visited Seneca Falls so often that the Stanton children began to call her "Aunt Susan." Mrs. Stanton's husband, Henry, summed up their relationship well when he said to his wife, "You stir up Susan, and she stirs up the world."

Chapter Five: 1851-1853
The Right to Speak

Dressed in a new outfit called "the bloomer," Susan and her friend Lucy Stone stepped out into the warm noon-hour sun to go to the post office. They were so lost in their thoughts that they didn't notice the boys following them until quite a crowd had gathered.

"Gradually we noticed that we were being encircled," Lucy wrote later. "A wall of men and boys at last shut us in, so that to go on or to go back was impossible. There we stood. The crowd was a good-natured one. They laughed at us. They made faces at us. They said impertinent things, and they would not let us out. Every moment brought added numbers, who peered over to see what attracted the crowd." A policeman came and broke up the crowd, and the women continued on their way with a sigh of relief.

Susan had to admit that her new outfit took some getting used to. With a pair of long pants under a skirt that ended just below the knee, it made so much more sense than the long dresses, petticoats, and hoops that women of the 1850s usually wore. She no longer had to worry about holding her skirts to keep them from dragging in snow or mud, getting caught in doors, or tripping her.

In 1851, Elizabeth Stanton encouraged women to wear the
bloomer costume. Susan B. Anthony, who also wore
the bloomer for many months, suffered much teasing
and mockery because of it.
Library of Congress

Susan B. Anthony And Justice For All

The bloomer caused a scene wherever women wore it. In 1851 most women never showed their legs or even talked about them; they called them "limbs" instead. So even though the bloomer covered a woman's legs, it made it obvious that she *had* legs — and this was considered very improper.

Mrs. Stanton favored the bloomer, too. She complained, "For us commonplace, everyday working characters who wash and iron, bake and brew, carry water and fat babies upstairs and down, bring potatoes, apples, and pans of milk from the cellar, run our own errands through mud or snow, shovel paths and work in the garden, why, 'the drapery' [long skirts] is too much — one might as well work with a ball and chain."

Mrs. Stanton insisted on the most amazing ideas in a way that made them seem perfectly reasonable. Within a short time after their first introduction, she persuaded Susan to abandon her quiet Quaker dresses in favor of the bloomer. Susan wore the unusual outfit for twelve long months when she campaigned hard for temperance and women's rights throughout New York State.

This took quite a bit of courage. It was one thing to wear the bloomer in Seneca Falls, where Mrs. Stanton and her friends talked regularly about women wearing sensible clothing, having their own money, and divorcing husbands who drank too much. But in some of the towns where Susan journeyed, people still took it for granted that good women managed their households quietly and didn't stir things up with talk of equality for women.

Susan B. Anthony And Justice For All

Unfortunately, Susan did not look very attractive in the bloomer. It made her seem even taller than she was and accented the leanness of her body. To make matters worse, the serious expression on her face just invited teasing and mockery. If only she could have met them with Mrs. Stanton's jolly smile and confident attitude, wearing the bloomer would have been so much easier.

The staring and rude comments greeted her outfit everywhere except in Rochester, where people kept quiet because they respected her father and brother. Finally she gave up the outfit, saying sadly that the bloomer fixed people's attention on her clothing instead of on her words. For the rest of her life, she usually chose plain, dark dresses for her public speeches, saving the bright colors she loved for home.

Even after they stopped wearing the bloomer, Susan and her temperance friends constantly fought against the idea that women should remain silent in public. Women had suffered so much because of men's drinking; why shouldn't they speak of it? In that time women seldom drank, but they often made beer, wine, and liquor at home for their husbands, and the alcohol could be very strong.

Mrs. Stanton also disapproved of alcohol. As the daughter of a judge, she had grown up listening to sad stories of women whose drunken husbands had lost their jobs and beat their wives and children. Laws had to be changed so that men confused by drink could not take sons and daughters, property, and money away from women. These changes made sense to Susan.

Susan B. Anthony And Justice For All

The more she talked about the evils of alcohol, the more she recognized the sufferings of women, and she began to speak more about woman's rights. This story, told in Susan's own words, tells of the quiet desperation that woman were enduring all over the country every day:

"We stopped at a little tavern where the landlady was not yet twenty and had a baby 15 months old. Her supper dishes were not washed and her baby was crying....She rocked the little thing to sleep, washed the dishes and got our supper....She gave us her warm bedroom to sleep in, and on a row of pegs hung the loveliest embroidered petticoats and baby clothes, all the work of that young woman's fingers, while on a rack was her ironing perfectly done. She prepared six o'clock breakfast for us....Now when we came to pay our bill, the dolt of a husband took the money and put it in his pocket. He had not lifted a hand to lighten that woman's burdens, but had sat and talked with the men in the bar room, not even caring for the baby, yet the law gives him the right to every dollar she earns."

In 1852, Susan was sent by her women's group, the Daughters of Temperance, to an Albany meeting led by men who were also against drinking. She took her place with the other ladies, who were expected to listen in silence. After awhile, however, she felt she just had to say something. The man in charge replied, "The sisters were not invited here to speak but to listen and learn."

She strode out angrily and called her own meeting. A few weeks later when women were silenced at another temperance gathering run by men, she again held her own meeting, which attracted more people than the men's group!

That year, Susan started a large organization called the Women's State Temperance Society. With two other women, she set an ambitious goal: to visit thirty counties in New York State to get people to sign a petition and to ask New York State to pass a law to limit the sale of liquor. It was the first of many such campaigns, and they succeeded in obtaining 28,000 signatures.

Now Susan was beginning to agree with Mrs. Stanton that women should be able to vote. In 1853, only White men could do so. Neither Black men nor any woman had a say in which ideas became law. Susan told her listeners that women should advise their husbands, sons, and brothers to vote for a law against alcohol, and if the men would not do so, women should vote for themselves.

By now women had shown that they could do more at temperance meetings than "listen and learn"; they could hold their own gatherings, give their own convincing speeches, and gain thousands of names asking for better laws. More than 2,000 people attended the 1852 Woman's Rights Convention in Syracuse, and the newspaper in that city said, "No person can deny that there was a greater amount of talent in the woman's rights convention than has characterized any public gathering in this city during the last ten years."

Still, a male minister spoke for many people of that time when he said that a woman was out of place taking such an active role. "She should cast her eyes down when meeting men, drop her veil when walking up the aisle of a church and keep her place at home."

The following January, Susan presented all the petitions to the New York Legislature, where the state laws were made. However, this did not impress the lawmakers, who scoffed, "Who are these asking for a law against alcohol? Nobody but women and children!"

Chapter Six: 1854-1860
The Perils of Public Life

Susan stopped working the farm and settled into the traveling lifestyle that she followed until she was a silver-haired woman. Using Rochester as a home base, she traveled regularly to speak about temperance. At first she supported herself with money she had saved from her teaching career, but as she became more well-known, she was able to charge audiences a fee to attend the meetings she organized. Sometimes wealthy friends who appreciated her work simply gave her money. Occasionally, when expenses were greater than ticket sales, she borrowed money from her family.

If lawmakers had paid attention to Susan when she spoke about the dangers of strong alcohol, she might never have felt the urge to strive to get the vote for women. But society refused to listen to her well-reasoned arguments about temperance just because she was a woman. Eventually, she realized that the best way to make herself heard on this or any other topic was to vote. After all, if women were able to elect politicians into office, they could also vote them out of office. Knowing this, politicians would begin listening to women so they could keep their jobs. So starting in

1854, Susan and the other reformers went each year to the state legislature, presenting petitions that married women might keep their own earnings and have the right to say what happened to their children.

After the lawmakers ignored the petitions the first time, Susan's group decided to take the message of married women's rights face-to-face to the people of New York. Susan organized meetings in every county in the state, and conducted more than half of them by herself.

The winter of 1854-55 was one of the coldest and snowiest on record. Full-grown evergreen trees looked like Christmas village miniatures as snow covered them halfway to their top branches. When the snow was especially high, only half the street would be plowed, and they would travel between tall, narrow walls of white. Sometimes when the snow fell fine and wet, Susan could not keep it from making its way under her collar and down her neck. And whenever she strayed the least little bit off the shoveled paths, snow sneaked in over the top of her boots, soaking her stockings.

In those days, before the automobile, the quickest way to get from town to town was by railroad. Unfortunately, the train passed miles away from many of the small towns the reformers visited on their speaking tours. The only way to reach these villages in the winter was by sleigh.

To keep warm, Susan bought heavy, new boots. When she first wore them they felt fine, but they began to pinch when she hurried all around town putting up posters and making last-minute arrangements about the lecture hall. She got so busy that she didn't change out of them for several hours. By bedtime at the relatives' house where she was staying, her feet had swollen so much inside the boots that she could hardly take them off.

When she awoke early the next morning, the pain was no better. In fact, it was worse. Now it ran up her legs and into her back.

Her traveling companion knocked on Susan's door to see if she was ready.

When Susan opened her bedroom door, the other woman gasped. Susan usually walked so tall and straight; why was she now limping painfully with her shoulders bowed? She hadn't even coiled up her hair yet in her usual neat style.

Susan confided that she was having trouble with her boots and asked her cousin for help. Lowering herself carefully into a chair, Susan pulled at the top of her boot while her companion pushed on the sole.

Her cousin noted that Susan seemed to be having trouble with her feet and back. Was Susan really fit to travel?

More confidently than she looked, Susan nodded that she was fine. During breakfast, however, she sat as still as possible so her back wouldn't hurt any worse. In vain her relatives pleaded with her to stay and rest for a day. But Susan protested that she would go to Canton as long as she was still alive.

Finally, grateful for her relatives' concern, she allowed them to help her into the sleigh and tuck blankets around her.

Although the horses had barely started to trot off,

Newspapers often made fun of Susan B. Anthony. In this political cartoon drawn by Charles Lewis Bartholomew between 1892 and 1896, Susan B. Anthony is chasing President Grover Cleveland.
Library of Congress

Susan B. Anthony And Justice For All

Susan already felt frozen to the seat. Each rut in the road sent a knife of pain shooting from her toes up towards her neck. Shifting to another position only made it worse. The best way to bear the pain was to tuck her arms around her lower legs and rest her head on her knees. Seventeen miles later, when she arrived in the next town, she could hardly straighten up.

Susan went right ahead with all her speaking engagements that winter. Pain was her constant companion until the following fall, when she stopped for a three-month rest.

If physical suffering wouldn't keep Susan from speaking up for woman's rights, neither would the criticism of her abolitionist friends. When a homeless, unpopular woman named Mrs. Phelps needed help in 1860, Susan offered it bravely.

Mrs. Phelps was the wealthy mother of three children, married to a member of the Massachusetts Senate. She suspected him of loving another woman, and one day she told him so. He became so angry that he threw her down the stairs. The husband could not risk having people hear about his affair and his terrible temper, so he had his wife locked up in an asylum. For a year and a half, she lived like a prisoner, away from the children she loved.

Finally, she promised to stop talking about her husband's disturbing behavior. She was then allowed to leave the asylum to stay with her brother, who was a United States senator. How good it was to be free to move around and talk to people who were well! And how happy she was to have her children visit her! But when it came time for them to leave, Mrs. Phelps felt grief-stricken. She begged her brother to let her daughter stay longer.

Her brother replied, "It is of no use for you to say another word. The child belongs by law to the father...If you make any more trouble about it we'll send you back to the asylum."

When her brother wasn't looking, Mrs. Phelps fled with her daughter to Quaker friends, who introduced them both to Susan. No one else wanted to shelter this desperate woman whose brother and husband were both famous lawmakers. Because these men were so powerful, they could throw someone in jail for helping Mrs. Phelps. After all, according to the law, Mrs. Phelps had "stolen" her own daughter away from the child's father.

Susan agreed to help Mrs. Phelps and her child. Disguising them in old clothes and Mrs. Phelps in green goggles, she boarded a train with them on Christmas afternoon.

In a way, Mrs. Phelps fared no better than a slave fleeing by means of the Underground Railroad. Just as the slaves were imprisoned and made to endure physical cruelty, so Mrs. Phelps was imprisoned and made to endure mental cruelty. Neither women nor Black people were free in 1860, and Susan intended to do something about both situations.

Susan took the mother and daughter to New York City to hide them with people she knew. Because it was late at night when they arrived, Susan tried to get a hotel room for the night. However, the clerk refused to rent a room to them. After Susan threatened to sleep in the lobby, he gave in. The whole next day Susan took Mrs. Phelps and her daughter from one home to another, but no one would help them for fear of breaking the law.

At that time Susan was working hard against slavery, and the other abolitionists advised her to have nothing to do with the woman or it would make the antislavery workers look bad. Susan replied angrily, "Trust me that as I ignore all law to help the slave, so will I ignore it all to protect an enslaved woman."

That same year, New York State passed a law that granted women the right to say what happened to the money they earned and what happened to their children. It did Mrs. Phelps no good, however, because she was from a different state. After hiding successfully for a year and a half with another Quaker family, the mother allowed her daughter to go alone to Sunday school. Senator Phelps kidnapped the girl, and Mrs. Phelps never saw her again. Nothing more could be done by Susan or anyone else to help her.

This incident made Susan more sure than ever that she needed to work for woman's rights. Therefore, she was very discouraged when all the people who worked with her on this cause said, "The nation is being torn apart over the issue of slavery. Let's work to get the Negroes free."

Susan knew that laws are changed through the efforts of many people striving together. Without the support of others, even a reformer as strong as she could not accomplish woman's liberation all alone. So she gave most of her energy to the antislavery movement, resolving that she would come back to the woman's cause as soon as possible.

Chapter Seven: 1861-1864
Working Against Slavery

Susan had seen many angry crowds before, but this was one of the worst.

When all the other women had been escorted to safety outside the hall, she stood alone with the abolitionist men to face the rowdy audience. As a rotten egg flew toward the stage, she tried to appear calm. But as Reverend Samuel May struggled to continue his speech about the evils of slavery, a man in the audience stood hollering on a bench, "Down with abolitionists! They'll wreck the country!" A moment later, the seat was hauled out from under him and broken across his shoulders. Everywhere in the crowd pistols and knives gleamed with the promise of violence. The smell of whiskey made Susan want to cover her nose.

Now a man climbed clumsily onto the stage. Others quickly followed and roughly elbowed Reverend May out of the way. Stamping and clapping drunkenly, the men began to sing the Star Spangled Banner. Conducting the music with a gun, another yelled, "If you really love your country, sing!"

"I'll drink to that," several cheered, passing a bottle of whiskey around.

Susan B. Anthony And Justice For All

The crowd howled so loudly that Susan hardly noticed the police officer at her side, who urged her to leave before things got worse. Turning, she reluctantly followed Reverend Samuel May and the rest of her group out the door.

It was 1861, the year that Susan remembered afterwards as the winter of mobs. As she was in charge of the Antislavery Society speakers, she organized a series of lectures throughout New York State. Things had gone well enough in the small villages where there were too few people to riot. Larger cities like Syracuse, however, were so dangerous that Mrs. Stanton's husband urged them to quit.

The country was growing, and with it grew America's quarrel over slavery. As pioneers settled new lands in the West and South, people in those territories asked to become part of the United States (or the Union, as it was sometimes called). Territories and states in the South, where slavery was common, threatened to form their own government if they couldn't have unpaid Black workers. But the East and North were full of abolitionists who continued calling for the end of this great evil in society.

Even among themselves, the antislavery workers disagreed on some points. Should slavery be outlawed completely in all of the states? Should the states that already had slaves be allowed to keep them? Should new territories be allowed into the Union only if they promised not to have slaves?

Susan belonged to the group whose motto was, "No union with slaveholders," meaning that all slaves in

To show that they hated antislavery workers, this mob burned
dummies of Susan B. Anthony and her friend.

every state should be free. Territories should not become states unless they promised to outlaw slavery within their borders, they said. Furthermore, they thought that if a state already had slaves, it should give them up.

Some Northerners who bought cheap cotton and other goods from the South wanted slavery to continue — down South. Other Northerners argued that antislavery laws would tear the United States in two. In fact, that's just what happened: in April of 1861, the bloody, four-year Civil War broke out between the Northern and Southern states.

On the night of the mob in Syracuse, Susan and her band of speakers stayed at the home of a friend. The antislavery workers could hear the rioters from the nearby Convention Hall yelling in the streets. Even though the travelers were supposed to leave early the next morning, no one in the house could sleep. They peered through the darkness outside the window and prayed that the mob would not stop in front of the house.

But they did! Banging pans, swearing, and drinking, the angry rioters halted at the end of the walk. A tall man repeated the earlier cry of the evening, "Down with the abolitionists!" Behind him someone raised what looked like a man's body on a pole above the crowd.

Now the body of a woman in a long black dress was raised beside that of the man. All at once everyone in the room realized what was really on the poles: dummies! One was supposed to be Susan, the other Reverend May.

"We don't want any abolitionists around here," roared a rioter. "Now watch carefully, 'cause I'm gonna show you what'll happen to you if you don't leave town first thing tomorrow!" He and his friends yanked the dummies down to the street, threw them about, stomped on them, and finally dragged them away.

From the street corner, someone shouted, "And here's what we think of your temperance speeches, Miss Anthony!" As he poured whiskey all over the dummies, another man cried, "Burn 'em. Let's burn 'em in the square where everyone can see." Although she was too far away to see the flames, she could guess when the dummies caught fire because she heard the cheering from a distance.

Even this frightening experience didn't stop Susan from working for the abolition of slavery. Her usual routine that winter was to travel one day, then give two speeches the next; on and on, week after week, town after town. Sometimes her group would stay in hotels, but often they were able to lodge with others committed to antislavery.

There was one serious drawback to this generosity: the food. In this era of reforms, many people adopted strange diets because they wanted to purify their bodies as well as their souls. One well-to-do family, for example, served only nuts, apples, and coarse bread. This was not enough to keep weary, cold travelers energetic. Several of the men complained that they could not go on unless they got more food to eat.

Still other speakers refused to travel when the snow became deep and the temperature dropped below zero. Several of the best women, including Mrs. Stanton, frequently had to stay home to care for their young children. Susan certainly understood the importance of child-rearing, for she had often taken charge of all seven of Mrs. Stanton's children while her friend wrote speeches in her airy Seneca Falls home.

Even so, Susan felt very frustrated when family responsibilities forced her speakers to change their plans. One time, when several speakers kept asking her to rearrange the lecture schedule, she complained to a traveling companion, "O, dear, dear, how I do wish you could have kept on with me. I cannot tell you how utterly awful is the suspense these other women keep me in; first, they can't, then they can, then they won't unless things are so and so; and when I think everything is settled, it all has to be gone over again."

Susan had two reasons to dedicate herself so strongly to her antislavery tours. First, the Anthony family had opposed slavery for as long as she could remember. Back in the 1830s, when her father operated his mills successfully, he tried to buy cotton that was not grown by slaves. He said he hated supporting masters who forced others to work for free.

During the early years she taught, Susan had noted with disgust that the Quakers nearby would not let educated, free Black women pray downstairs in the Meeting House with everyone else, but insisted that they sit apart. Later that week she made a point to have tea with the women and befriend them. Soon afterwards, she wrote home, "I have had the unspeakable satisfaction of visiting four colored*

* In Susan's time, the words 'colored' and 'Negro' were considered respectful terms for African-Americans.

people and drinking tea with them....To show this kind of people respect in this heathen land affords me a double pleasure."

Second, Susan heard stories directly from several ex-slaves that impressed her deeply. Frederick Douglass told how slave masters sold young children to homes far away from their parents. Once he had seen a slavemaster "whip a woman, causing the blood to run half an hour at a time; and this, too, in the midst of her crying children, pleading for their mother's release." Slaves were not allowed to read because they might learn about their rights. When they escaped these awful plantations, their masters hunted them down with dogs. Slave hunters could earn $1,000 just by returning escaped Blacks to their owners.

Susan made friends with many courageous Black people who wanted their race to be free. At least twice she helped prepare runaway slaves for the last leg of the journey on the Underground Railroad. She also shared speakers' platforms with Sojourner Truth, a former slave who taunted her audiences: "We'll have our rights; see if we don't; and you can't stop us from them, see if you can."

In July 1863, President Lincoln freed slaves in all the Southern states that had dropped out of the Union. However, he allowed slavery to continue in other parts of the country. The war between North and South still dragged on, costing the country thousands of lives. To people like Susan and Mrs. Stanton, anything less than a total end to slavery was not enough.

Blotting out slavery completely presented a big

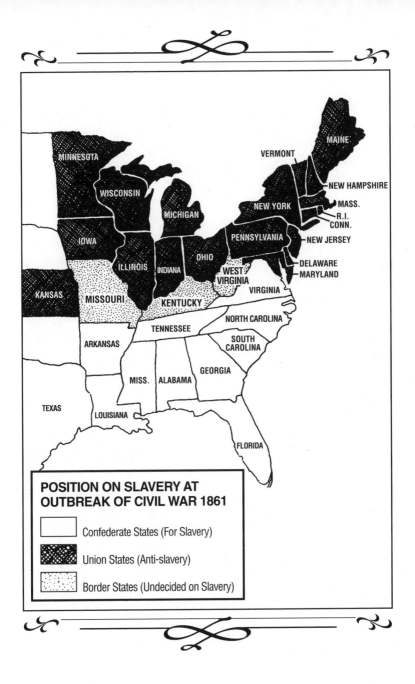

POSITION ON SLAVERY AT
OUTBREAK OF CIVIL WAR 1861

Confederate States (For Slavery)

Union States (Anti-slavery)

Border States (Undecided on Slavery)

challenge, for it was not outlawed in the Constitution of the United States, the highest law of the land. It would take another law to change (or amend) the Constitution to banish slavery.

Abolitionists thought long and hard about how to persuade Congress to change the Constitution.

"Why not try the same methods we used to persuade New York State to give rights to wives?" one of the women suggested. "This time we'd get people to sign petitions that they want slavery outlawed in every part of the country."

"Yes, that's a good idea, and it worked fine in New York," reasoned another. "However, the Constitution is a federal law that applies in every state. Therefore, we'd have to get signatures from every state. That would be a huge job!"

Susan was good at huge jobs, especially when she had Mrs. Stanton to write the letters and speeches to inspire people to take part. Soon the two sent out a letter to women of every state, saying, "Women, you can not vote or fight for your country. Your only way to be a power in the government is through the exercise of this one, sacred, constitutional 'right of petition;' and we ask you to use it now to the utmost. Go to the rich, the poor,...the white, the black — gather up the names of all who hate slavery...and lay them at the feet of Congress...."

To collect petitions, Susan and Mrs. Stanton helped form the Woman's National Loyal League. From her new office in New York City, Susan mailed letters far and wide, sent out lecturers to stir up townspeople, and found a job for every woman who offered to gather signatures. Under her direction, 2,000 members worked several months and succeeding in collecting the names of 400,000 people who hated slavery. These petitions were collected in huge sacks and dumped on the floor of Congress.

Susan devoted every moment she could to work for humanity. Still, she gave what time she could to her family. When her mother needed help putting on a wedding for Susan's brother Daniel, Susan went home. She grieved when her father died in 1862 and later when the family moved from the farm to a home on Madison Street in Rochester. To her sister Mary she wrote, "Your letter sent a pang to my very heart's core that the dear old home, so full of the memory of our father, must be given up....Every place, every movement, almost, suggests him."

In the midst of her war work and personal sadness came a letter from a man who had known her when she was younger. "Marry me," he wrote. Her diary does not explain why she refused him, but her other writings suggest that she preferred to continue her work rather than marry.

Finally, in the spring of 1865, the Civil War ended and Congress passed the Thirteenth Amendment to the Constitution outlawing slavery everywhere in the United States. How the abolitionists rejoiced! Congressman Charles Sumner praised Susan again and again, saying that the petitions she sent proved very helpful in persuading Congress to abolish slavery completely.

The Woman's National Loyal League helped win a tremendous victory. If Susan B. Anthony never did anything else, she could have counted herself a great woman just for her important role in securing freedom for millions of slaves. Once the Thirteenth Amendment passed, she closed the Loyal League headquarters and took a vacation to visit her brother Daniel in Kansas.

Chapter Eight: 1865-1868
Abolitionists Turn Their Backs

The late-afternoon sun streamed in through the office window. Despite the stifling August heat, Susan was enjoying Kansas, where she had been visiting Daniel and his family for several months.

The war was over. Now, although the North had won, the recently freed African-Americans had a new set of problems. Four days after the war's end, President Lincoln was shot and killed by a man who wanted the South to win. The new president, Andrew Johnson, was friendly with wealthy Southern landowners who had owned slaves.

Although the war had been fought to free the slaves, Johnson allowed the landowners to treat Black people very badly. Southern employers refused to hire Blacks, and the law said that if they didn't have steady jobs, they had to pay large fines. If they couldn't pay, they were forced to work without pay.

Susan thought deeply about these problems as she labored among the ex-slaves in Kansas. For several months, however, she also gave part of her time to new pursuits.

Her brother, who was mayor of Leavenworth, published the newspaper, The *Leavenworth Bulletin*.

When he was re-elected mayor, he plunged himself into rounds of speeches and meetings to win votes. Gladly he accepted Susan's help in managing the paper, asking that she not fill it solely with woman's rights and Black suffrage.

At the *Bulletin,* Susan learned the newspaper business. She delved into every detail of it: gathering and writing news; composing type (lining up the letters that make up the words); inking and running the presses. She gained confidence in her ability to manage large printed jobs. Best of all, though, was the satisfaction and pride she enjoyed when she saw readers reaching for her version of the day's events.

In the composing room, a White man bent over his work. Susan missed the Black printer who had done that job for a few days. Soon after she had hired him, however, all the other employees refused to work by his side. Daniel could not afford to lose all his workers, even though he believed strongly in the equality of both races. He was bitterly sad about having to fire the Black man. Susan did everything she could to help her friend find different work.

Would Father have made such a hiring mistake if he were still alive? Probably not. Now Susan was beginning to understand his long-ago refusal to hire a woman as an overseer in his mills. Well, even though she had lost this one small battle, she would not give up her larger effort to help Black people have a better life. She knew that her father, dead for two years, would have wished her to continue.

She disagreed strongly with some of her old antislavery heroes, who said that their work was done now that the slaves were freed. But freedom meant nothing to Blacks who could not vote to protect their rights, she thought. The same thing applied to women: they, too were free citizens but were silenced when it came to voting or making laws. The Antislavery Society had been talking for a long time about guaranteeing women's and African-Americans' rights by adding a Fourteenth Amendment to the Constitution. She hoped it would happen soon.

In Leavenworth, Susan took more time than usual to relax and enjoy Daniel's family. After years of campaigning for reform, it felt very good to stay in one house for several months. She enjoyed taking carriage rides, sewing, and visiting with the many interesting people who came to see her brother. She wrote in her diary, "I am afraid I shall get into the business of being comfortable."

The longer she stayed, the more urgent became the letters from back East. A good friend named Wendell Phillips said, "Why have you deserted the field of action at a time like this, at an hour unparalleled in almost 20 centuries? If you watch our papers you must have observed that with you gone, our forces are scattered...."

Mrs. Stanton begged, "Come home."

Although these letters disturbed her, Susan knew that she had important work to do in Kansas. She had visited schools for Black children and spoken to the teachers about the best way to help the students catch up on all the book learning they had missed as slaves. She also met with a group of Black men and women to help them form an Equal Rights League.

Susan B. Anthony And Justice For All

One afternoon Daniel walked into The *Leavenworth Bulletin* office, but Susan hardly noticed he was there. She had been reading the newspaper, and she could hardly believe what it said.

"All persons born or naturalized in the United States...are citizens of the United States....No State shall make or enforce any law which shall abridge the privileges...of citizens of the United States." This was the new Fourteenth Amendment that lawmakers planned to vote on. Yes, this was good news.

She breathed in the feeling of victory. Finally! Women citizens, who had been paying taxes all this time, would finally be allowed to vote. Blacks would too, of course.

Daniel read the amendment over her shoulder. Looking upset, he noted that it said nothing about guaranteeing women the right to vote.

She assured him that women were included. All those years when women were campaigning for the vote for Blacks, the Antislavery Society was talking about universal suffrage — the vote for every citizen — women too. It was always the goal to win suffrage for everyone at once.

Daniel shook his head sadly and pointed out that they were saying something different now. They were suggesting that states who refused any *male* the right to vote should be punished, but they did not say anything about women.

Susan set her lips tight. "I must get back East and straighten this out," she said, and she left as soon as she could. Arriving back in her home state, she spent a night at Mrs. Stanton's mapping out the campaign that was to keep her busier than ever for the next 30 years of her life.

First she went to all her old abolitionist friends and asked them to help persuade Congress to give the vote to women. For awhile her co-workers seemed to agree that this should be done, suggesting that the Fourteenth Amendment would do its job better if the word *male* were simply removed. (They wanted it to say that states who refused any *citizen* the right to vote should be punished. This would include both men and women.)

As time went on, however, one man after another in the Antislavery Society began to argue with the woman who had worked so hard to free the slaves. Some abolitionists said that Americans might approve an amendment giving Blacks the vote, but they would be likely to reject the document if it also included the vote for women. It would be better, they said, to get Black men the vote and try again for women in another 20 years or so.

Even Mrs. Stanton's cousin, the abolitionist Gerrit Smith, turned against woman's rights. "This is the time to settle the rights of races; unless we do justice to the Negro we shall bring down on ourselves another bloody revolution, another four years' war, but we have nothing to fear from woman, she will not avenge herself."

Wendell Phillips, an important leader of the Antislavery Society, argued that they should not strike out the word *male* from the proposed amendment.

"I would sooner cut off my right hand than ask the

ballot for the black man and not for woman," Susan retorted, then bitterly turned on her heel and marched out of the office.

Horace Greeley, the powerful editor of the New York *Tribune,* had been a faithful supporter of universal suffrage for years. Now, however, he sided with those who preferred to extend the vote to only Black men. More times than Susan and Mrs. Stanton could count, they heard him say, "The best women I know do not want to vote." So while the two women traveled New York State gathering petitions for women to vote, they paid a quiet visit to Mary Cheney Greeley, the editor's wife. A long-time supporter of woman's rights, Mary agreed to help in a special way.

Even to present their petitions, the woman reformers were not allowed to speak at the New York State Constitutional Convention, so they prepared George William Curtis to speak for them. Addressing Greeley, Curtis said, "I hold in my hand a petition from Mrs. Horace Greeley and 300 other women citizens...asking that the word 'male' be stricken from the Constitution." Even though Greeley blushed with embarrassment, he stubbornly went ahead and persuaded the convention to vote against female suffrage.

Greeley never forgot how the women had tried to outsmart him. A few weeks later when he saw Susan and Mrs. Stanton at a friend's house, he walked up to them and said angrily, "You two ladies are the most maneuvering politicians in the State of New York. I saw in the manner my wife's petition was presented, that Mr. Curtis was acting under instructions, and I saw the reporters prick up their ears."

Not only did New York State refuse the vote to women, but soon after that the Fourteenth Amendment passed, keeping the word *male*.

Despite the failure to persuade New Yorkers to let women vote, Susan and Mrs. Stanton still hoped that other individual states would grant this right. Kansas lawmakers planned to discuss this very idea soon. Lending support to that state's campaign, the two reformers started their journey westward immediately.

If 1861 was the winter of mobs, then the 1867 Kansas trip was the summer of bedbugs. Susan could hardly sleep because of the insects; in the morning, she said, "we picked a thousand out of the ruffles of our dresses." As they faced the hardships of travel in that frontier state, they missed their comfortable bloomer outfits. Their clothing seemed caked with dust as they bumped along over poor roads in open wagons; when crossing streams and rivers without bridges, it proved hard to keep their many petticoats and long skirts dry. The carriage ride on one part of the trip was so hard that it killed a pair of Indian horses and two ponies.

Despite the riots during the winter of mobs, Susan had been able to rely on other antislavery members for support and encouragement. On this trip, however, she and Mrs. Stanton suffered many painful reminders that people who used to work for woman's vote were now putting them aside in favor of the Black movement. It made the journey much harder.

When a wealthy man named George Francis Train

offered to help them campaign for women, they gladly accepted. However, their abolitionist friends, and even their woman's rights supporters, warned them not to get involved with him.

"George Francis Train!" they exclaimed. "That crackpot? He draws as much attention for his flashy clothes and ridiculous habits as he does for his beliefs. He'll make a laughingstock of you!" Since most of the more respectable people would not help in Kansas, however, Susan and Mrs. Stanton included him on their speaking tour. Besides, they knew from their experience with bloomers that ridiculous habits and unusual clothing were sometimes signs of a valuable ally.

Almost immediately they ran into trouble with Mr. Train. Once he learned that his male traveling companion had decided to go hunting instead, Train took a closer look at the route the women had mapped out. Then he stated that the trip was too rough for any man and since Mr. Reynolds had deserted him, he would give up the tour.

However, Susan would not let him get away with this. "The engagements have been made," she said, "and hand-bills were sent to every post office within 50 miles of the towns where meetings are to be held....I shall take Mr. Reynolds' place. At one o'clock I shall send a carriage to your hotel." And even though unmarried ladies were not supposed to travel alone with gentlemen, that is exactly what she did.

During one long journey, Mr. Train asked Susan why there was no newspaper devoted to woman's rights. She replied that she had often wanted to publish one, but didn't have enough money.

That evening the wealthy Mr. Train astonished his traveling companion. "When Miss Anthony gets back to New York," he announced to the crowd, "she is going to start a woman suffrage paper. Its name is to be the *Revolution*...its editors will be Elizabeth Cady Stanton and Parker Pillsbury....Let everybody subscribe for it!" He offered to help pay for the paper and introduced Susan to his partner David Mellis.

Susan felt glad that he hadn't asked her to write the newspaper herself. Father and Mother meant well by sending her to study at Miss Moulson's, but her prim teacher never taught Susan how to write well. Miss Moulson was so concerned about how pupils dotted their i's and crossed their t's that she made Susan afraid of putting pen to paper. Only in her journal and letters to friends could she write without feeling ashamed.

They left Kansas shortly after the votes for the state amendment about woman suffrage were counted. Only 9,000 voters of the 30,000 cast their ballot for this cause. Because this was the very first time lawmakers had ever considered women's issues important enough to vote on, Susan still felt encouraged. She would continue to fight, and now she would have her own newspaper to spread her views to more people.

Chapter Nine: 1868-1870
Susan Publishes a Newspaper

A newspaper of their own! Supporters of the woman's movement had tried to get a paper together for a long time, and now it was finally happening. The newspaper was part of Susan's dream to have a big printing business that published its own daily news. All the work would be done by women. In this way wealthy, educated women could open new professions to other females.

Susan and Mrs. Stanton were very pleased about their new challenge; however, other woman's activists continued to write cutting letters advising them not to have anything to do with Mr. Train. Not only was he a dandy, he also disliked Black people! In spite of all criticism, however, the first edition of the *Revolution* rolled off the presses in January 1868.

Susan and Mrs. Stanton settled into the comfortable pattern that had by now become very familiar. Mrs. Stanton described their relationship in this way: "In writing we did better work together than either could alone. While she is slow in composition, I am rapid....I am the better writer, she the better critic. She supplied the facts and statistics, I the philosophy and rhetoric, and together we have made arguments that have stood unshaken by the storms of 30 long years."

Besides supplying information, Susan also managed the office, paid the bills, worked with the printers, and distributed the paper every week.

However, paying the bills turned out to be more difficult than planned. As soon as the first edition was off the press, Train left for Ireland, where he spent a year in jail for interfering in the government. During that time, he continued to send his articles but could not provide the money he had promised.

As publisher, Susan had two other ways to earn money from the *Revolution*. First, she signed up many subscribers, who paid $2 to receive a year's worth of copies. She also tried to persuade businesses to pay a fee to place ads in the paper. But soon she discovered that attracting advertisers was the hardest job of all. Some business owners criticized that the articles in the paper called for too much change too soon, while others said that they had already advertised in the other papers.

When Susan discussed these problems with friends, a few of them loaned her money because they thought the *Revolution* was a good newspaper. Still, there was never enough, even though she and Mrs. Stanton refused to take a penny for their work.

The *Revolution* did not make its owners rich. However, it did offer a wonderful opportunity to get people talking about justice for women and Blacks, and Susan aimed to make the best of it. Now almost 50 years old, she lived in New York City close to Mrs. Stanton. As she continued traveling, organizing conventions, and speaking, she told everyone about her newspaper. In turn, she used the paper to encourage people to attend the conventions and write about the speeches made there.

Susan spoke in every imaginable forum. She lectured at post offices and town halls, on crudely erected platforms and packing crates, and in smoky meeting rooms and opera houses. One occasion always made her smile whenever she recalled it: she was speaking on a platform and a baby sat with her mother in the front row. The audience sat so close to the platform that the baby could reach up and pinch Susan's ankles. Naturally, this made Susan uncomfortable and she tried to discourage it. However, every time Susan dodged the pinching, the little one cried. Rather than compete with the child's wailing, Susan endured the pinching until the lecture was over.

Both Susan and her newspaper frequently discussed the new Fifteenth Amendment that lawmakers wanted to pass. It gave United States citizens the right to vote regardless of their race or color, but not of their sex. How dare they give the vote to Blacks and ignore women? She protested at a meeting of the American Equal Rights Association, which had been formed with the intention of getting the vote for African-Americans and women.

Frederick Douglass asked members of the Association to support the amendment enthusi-astically. Susan was filled with rage. To help free the Negros only to have them turn around and ask for more rights than women had...Oh! it was so unfair!

Susan B. Anthony And Justice For All

No, don't support it, protested Susan, because it did not mean equal rights. Rather, she said, "it puts 2,000,000 men in the position of tyrants over 2,000,000 colored women." How could men even look women in the face, she continued, when they ask us to put the rights of Black men before any woman? After this, Susan was often accused of being anti-Negro, but she wasn't. She simply wanted all women to have the same privileges as Black men.

The *Revolution* also contained many articles about Abby McFarland. Her story proved once again how women needed more rights to protect them from husbands who hurt women and children and refused to share the family money.

Abby had married Daniel McFarland, who drank too much, abused her, and spent all his money on himself, forcing her to work. In those days there were few ways for women to earn money; many people considered it shameful for a woman to work outside the home. Besides, no matter how hard a woman worked, she could seldom bring home more than half of what a man would earn for doing the same job.

Abby fell in love with a kind and responsible man named Albert D. Richardson. They planned to get married as soon as she could divorce her alcoholic husband. A few days after the divorce, however, the enraged McFarland strode into Richardson's office and shot him. Abby's new love died a few hours later.

When McFarland was arrested for murder, the judge declared him innocent, saying that he had lost his mind. Worse yet, he was given custody of his and Abby's 12-year-old son, and let out of jail!

In New York City, where Susan lived and published her paper, women felt furious. Even if McFarland was insane and not simply drunk as usual, why let him have the child? He should be locked up so he couldn't hurt anyone else — especially his own boy. Because she had fallen in love with a man who was not her husband, many other people blamed Abby for creating the whole problem in the first place.

Susan gathered 2,000 women for a meeting, where Mrs. Stanton gave a powerful speech. By the time the meeting was over, the women decided to send a letter to the governor. The letter asked that McFarland be placed in a hospital for the insane and Abby be given back her child.

Naturally, the *Revolution* gave a full report of Abby's story, taking her side against her cruel husband. Susan and Mrs. Stanton received much criticism for taking the poor woman's side. However, for several weeks afterwards they received letters from other unhappy wives all over the country, who thanked them for supporting women like Abby.

Susan struggled so hard with the constant criticism and the newspaper's debts that even her family began to doubt whether she should continue. Her brother Daniel urged her to cut expenses by putting out the paper less often, but she would not. Her younger sister Mary spent most of the summer helping with the paper while Susan lectured and recruited subscribers.

Mary lamented to Susan: "You can not begin to know how you have changed....I beg of you for your own sake and for ours, do not persevere in this work unless people will aid you enough....It is very sad for all of us to feel that you are working so hard and being so misunderstood, and we constantly fear that, in some of your hurried business transactions, your enemies will delight to pick you up and make you still more trouble."

What Mary feared came true. Some of the Equal Rights Association members accused Susan of misusing their funds during her Kansas tour. Susan went back through all the records, proving where each dollar had been spent. However, being suspected like that during such a hard time was almost too much to bear.

Her dedication to her newspaper would not let her quit until the debts became too large to continue. As she said in this letter to a dear supporter:

"My paper must not, shall not go down....We only need time to win financial success. I know you will save me from giving the world a chance to say, 'There is a woman's rights failure; even the best of women can't manage business.' If I could only die, and thereby fail honorably, I would say 'amen,' but to live and fail — it would be too terrible to bear."

But live and fail she did. Susan was forced to sell her newspaper in 1870 for one dollar to another woman. Because the new owner was not a suffragist, she filled it with sweet poetry and other non-suffrage writing, as well as fashion. Susan wrote in her journal, "It was like signing my own death-warrant."

Susan's newspaper ended — but her responsibility for its debts dragged on. She was stuck with the remaining $10,000 in bills owed. Mrs. Stanton would not help with the debt, arguing that she needed every penny she earned to pay for her daughters' college educations. Instead, she suggested that Susan borrow money from her family (which she had already done) or get a job to pay for it all herself.

In those days, $10,000 was a huge amount of money — enough to buy three or four nine-room houses. Nevertheless, only a few days after she turned the paper over to its new editor, she started working hard to pay back the debt all by herself. It took her six years of lecturing to earn the money, and threw a shadow across her warm friendship with Mrs. Stanton for quite awhile.

Although Susan grieved about having to stop publishing her paper, she did not regret starting it in the first place. "I am not complaining, for mine is but the fate of almost every...pioneer who ever has opened up a way," she said.

Chapter Ten: 1872
Arrested for Being a Woman

After all the hustle-bustle of New York City, how quietly the streets of Rochester led her home.

Susan paused several weeks in her travels during the fall of 1872 to stay with her family on Madison Street. Several months before she received the news that her oldest sister Guelma had caught tuberculosis, a serious disease that was usually fatal. She wanted to spend time with Guelma, but she also had another purpose in mind: to find out what would happen when a woman actually tried to vote.

She made careful preparations before taking this important step. First she talked to retired Judge Henry R. Selden, who assured her that she would not be breaking the law by voting. After all, the Fourteenth Amendment did say that everyone born in the United States was a citizen; the law protected every citizen's right to vote. Although the amendment specifically said males had their rights protected, it did not deny that females did, too. Rather, it simply said nothing about females. She determined to "test" the amendment.

With this in mind, she gathered her sisters and went to the barbershop where voters (all men) in her

Susan B. Anthony And Justice For All

district registered. When she, Guelma, Hannah, and Mary approached, the inspectors in charge objected that women were not allowed to register or cast a ballot. Susan then read the Fourteenth Amendment to the United States Constitution, noting that it did not deny woman the right to vote. Reluctantly, the men registered the women.

By afternoon, the newspapers were already calling for the arrest of the inspectors for allowing the women to register. Susan hurried back to the barbershop to reassure them that, should they be arrested, she would take care of any legal costs. The next day, 35 other women in Rochester also signed up to vote.

On the morning of election day, Susan rose earlier than usual. Soon she and her sisters trooped two blocks down Main Street to vote. Susan kept the pace slow enough for Guelma, who coughed a lot when she became too tired. They had decided to go early in the morning to avoid making a scene. As planned, everything proceeded quietly. Later that day, eleven other women from their neighborhood voted.

That evening, she wrote a hasty letter to her best friend, "Well, I have been and gone and done it!! Positively voted the Republican ticket — straight — this A.M. at 7 o'clock and swore in my vote at that. Not a jeer, not a rude word, not a disrespectful look has met one woman....I hope you too voted."

Altogether, 50 women voted in Rochester that day. However, the inspectors were so frightened by the flurry of criticism in the newspapers that they counted only the votes of Susan B. Anthony and her 14 companions.

Susan B. Anthony And Justice For All

This time, newspapers all over the United States reported with great interest on how the women's votes had been accepted. Some contained mocking cartoons. But another editor wrote that if Judge Selden thought it was all right for Susan to vote, then she ought to have done it.

A few days later on a cloudy November afternoon, Susan rocked in her favorite chair in the family kitchen. Earlier that day she had raked up most of the leaves from the grape vines in the narrow side yard. Now she read the newspaper while Mary prepared for her next day's duties at school. Guelma was resting upstairs, her cough mercifully quiet for awhile.

The house was so peaceful that Susan jumped when the doorbell rang. But then she went back to her paper, knowing that Mary would answer the door.

Susan looked up in surprise when she heard her younger sister's footsteps approaching. Through the front hall, then the back parlor, then the dining room, and finally into the kitchen echoed the footsteps, bearing news of an uninvited visitor.

When Susan finally saw the expression on Mary's face, she forgot her reading completely.

What was wrong? Who was it?

"There's a Marshal Keeney to see you, Susan," Mary announced.

Susan rose, straightened her skirts, and took a deep breath. Retracing her sister's steps to the front hall, she remembered the events of the past few weeks. If this had happened sooner, she would have been more prepared. By now, she thought the issue had been settled in her favor.

She surveyed the tall gentleman who fiddled nervously with the high hat in his hands. "Good afternoon," she said, waiting calm and dignified.

The man shifted uncomfortably from one foot to the other and glanced shyly down at the tall, dark-haired woman. She hardly looked like a criminal. Why, she reminded him of an elderly woman he knew who always offered cookies when he visited as a boy. He blushed. This was a darn hard job. Silence gathered like dry leaves in the parlor, and his voice sounded too loud.

"Miss Anthony, it is my job on behalf of the United States government..." He cleared his throat. "That is, the commissioner wishes to arrest you," he finished in a rush.

Well, if I'm going to be arrested, they can at least treat me like a proper criminal instead of a harmless spinster, she thought. "Is this your usual method of serving a warrant?" she demanded, glaring at him.

"Oh, um...no." The marshal pulled a bunch of folded papers from his pocket and stood as tall as he could. "I have here a warrant for your arrest for voting in the presidential election in the eighth ward in Rochester, New York on November 5, 1872. Now if you'll just come with me, ma'am, I'll show you the way."

"I am not dressed to go to court," she said in a queenly manner.

He had heard plenty of excuses before, but hers seemed entirely out of place. This proper woman looked as if she always had her quiet clothing in complete order and her hair smoothly combed. Still, ladies would be ladies. Who knew how long she would take getting ready? Well, he didn't want to wait in this quiet room another moment.

"Oh, then just come on down to the courthouse when you are ready."

"Voting is not a crime, Mr. Keeney; I have broken no laws. Surely, under these circumstances, you do not think I would take myself down to the courthouse on my own!" He sighed, shifted to the other foot, and told her to accompany him as soon as she was ready.

When Susan returned in her hat and traveling cloak, she held out her wrists to be handcuffed. In a few hours, she knew, the newspapers would be hungry for every detail of this event. If the United States were really going to arrest a woman for voting, she wanted to give the press a good story.

Surprised, the marshal stepped back from her gloved hands. He really didn't need to handcuff her, he objected. What a long ride it would be on the streetcar with this woman!

When Marshal Keeney escorted Susan to the commissioner's office, she learned that all 14 of her fellow women voters, as well as the inspectors, had also been arrested.

When the women were told to pay $500 bail, Susan shook her head. She knew that people who refused bail were usually put in prison, and a woman in jail would gain sympathy for woman's rights in every part of the country.

She didn't mind spending a few days in a cell to win the vote for women. Anyway, after all she had endured for this cause — the mobs, freezing sleigh rides, and bedbugs — jail would probably seem comfortable. Once she was a prisoner, her case could be tried in the Supreme Court, if she lost in a lower court. She thought she had a good chance of eventually winning her case in the Supreme Court.

After her arrest, she hired Judge Henry Selden as her lawyer. She couldn't think of a better person to prepare her for prison and a trial in the highest court in the United States. He seemed to understand that she was willing to get arrested to find out whether the Fourteenth Amendment really did prevent women from voting. But Susan resented some of Selden's efforts to help. She was horrified several weeks later to discover that Selden had paid her bail. She immediately tried to take the money back, but could not get it from the courts.

Bitterly disappointed, she said to Selden, "Did you not know that you had stopped me from carrying my case to the Supreme Court?"

"Yes," he replied, "but I could not see a lady I respected put in jail."

He's trying to protect me because I'm a lady, she fumed inwardly. Doesn't he realize that such "protection" keeps women from having the right to take care of themselves? Now I will lose my chance to appeal my case to the Supreme Court.

Her trial was first scheduled for May 13 in Monroe County. She made good use of her time until that date, voting in the city election without any problems, as well as organizing and speaking at a number of conventions throughout the country. Beginning March 11, she lectured about a woman's constitutional right to vote in all 29 post office districts in her county.

Many of the people in these towns and neighborhoods had already heard Susan. Years before she had faced their teasing for her bloomer outfit, knocked on their doors asking for support of the Married Woman's Property Act, and braved angry crowds to talk about freeing the slaves. Now she stood before them talking about her upcoming trial for voting, a thing no woman had done before.

Some townspeople nodded, others frowned as they listened to her discussion of the United States Constitution. Her arguments were easy to follow, and her clear, musical voice carried easily above the noise of the street. Even those who disagreed with Susan B. Anthony admired her courage and intelligence.

Because Susan spoke with so many townspeople, she was starting to influence the opinions of the people who would make up the jury. The District Attorney, whose assignment was to argue that Susan was guilty, considered this unfair, so he rescheduled her trial for June 17 and moved it to the city of Canandaigua, in nearby Ontario County. Now, none of the people she had addressed in Monroe County could take part in her jury.

Susan B. Anthony, seated with two friends,
was sentenced by Judge Ward Hunt, who wouldn't
even let her speak at her own trial.

Chapter Eleven: 1873-1875

Guilty!

The District Attorney had ruined all her hard work to win people's favor in the county where her trial would be held. At this point, many strong people would have admitted defeat, but not Susan B. Anthony. She and Matilda Joslyn Gage simply laid out a map of Ontario County and scheduled themselves to speak in 37 of its meeting places. She gave the same speech so many times that she knew it by heart. The night before the trial, the woman reformers finished up their lecture tour in Canandaigua, where they gained support from an enthusiastic audience.

So many people were interested in her trial that the courtroom was jammed with spectators. Even ex-President Millard Fillmore sat in the stuffy room fanning himself. Judge Ward Hunt heard the arguments from both sides. However, he would not allow Susan to testify on her own behalf because she was a woman. For three hours Selden argued for Susan's innocence, claiming that her only real crime was being a woman. If she had been a man, she would have been praised for voting! Also, the laws affected women as much as men. Women cared as much about laws as did their husbands, brothers, and fathers, her lawyer continued, so why shouldn't women be allowed to vote for lawmakers?

After the District Attorney argued against Susan's political action for two hours, Judge Hunt took a piece of paper from his pocket and read his opinion that Susan had knowingly broken the law. Susan fumed silently, hardly believing what she was hearing. Since Hunt had not left his seat in court, everyone could tell that he had written his judgment before he had even heard all of the evidence.

Then he did something even more unbelievable. The jury was supposed to have a chance to debate her case among themselves. But the judge told them to say that she was guilty without even a discussion!

Shocked, Susan's lawyer jumped up and shouted, "Your Honor, I protest! Citizens who are accused of a crime are entitled by law to a trial by jury. I insist that you allow the jury to give their own verdict."

Hunt ignored the angry murmuring in the courtroom. Turning to the recording clerk, he said, "Write the verdict." Then he announced, "The jury is dismissed." Not one of them had been allowed to speak.

Because Susan had not received a fair trial, Selden demanded that she be given a new one. Hunt refused. Just before telling her what her punishment would be, the judge turned to the silent woman.

"Does the prisoner have anything to say?" he asked Susan.

Did she ever! Even though she had already lost her case, Susan took the opportunity to give him an earful. She stood up and began, "Your denial of my citizen's right to vote is the denial of my right of representation as one of the taxed, the denial of my right to a trial by a jury of my peers, and therefore the denial of my sacred right to life, liberty, property, and..."

"The Court can not allow the prisoner to go on," Hunt interrupted.

Boldly, Susan objected, "But your Honor will not deny me this one and only poor privilege of protest..." And she continued speaking in a voice that rang throughout the courtroom.

"Sit down!" Hunt almost shouted, losing patience. But she had overcome louder, angrier protesters before, so she took her time saying her piece. Finally she concluded by saying that as long as the judge had given her an unfair trial, he might as well give her a strict penalty to go along with it.

She shut her mouth firmly, sat down, and waited. Perhaps she had taunted him into sending her to jail after all. If he sent her to prison until the fine was paid, she could appeal her case to the Supreme Court.

Judge Hunt, however, recognized her attempt to reach the high court. Instead, he fined her only $100.

Through tight lips Susan replied, "May it please your Honor, I will never pay a dollar of your unjust penalty."

Susan had spent three months speaking in two counties and two hard days at her own trial. But she could not go home yet. Judge Hunt was scheduled to try the three voting inspectors, and had called her as a witness.

On the day of the inspectors' trial, she once again

sat helpless as the unfair judge refused to allow the jury to consider the matter. "Bring in a verdict of guilty," he ordered them. They did. The inspectors' lawyer, however, advised the men not to pay their fines.

As on the day of her arrest, Susan made the most of the whole unjust trial. She had 8,000 copies made of a written version of the actual trial and all that was said in her defense. These she gave to lawyers, libraries, newspapers, and anyone who would read them.

Her debts for the *Revolution* lay heavy on her mind. Her trial had taken up a whole year, and any money she earned during that time had to be used for hotels, carriages, and so on. Besides, she felt she could not leave home. Her sister Guelma lay dying, and Susan wanted to care for her.

The Anthony women had remained close all of their lives. For the past eight years, Guelma's family lived with Mary and Susan on Madison Street. Their 80-year-old mother, a widow ever since they had left the farm, was so upset by her oldest daughter's illness that she could hardly think. Mary worked a full-time job as a school principal, so she had to be away from home every day. Susan gladly took on the heaviest burden of caring for the sick woman.

In order to tend Guelma day and night, Susan refused all invitations to speak. She propped pillows behind her sister so that she might breathe more easily, but Guelma coughed so long and so hard that eventually she choked on her own blood. By November she was dead, and so were two other friends who had voted with Susan. Susan felt very alone as the women who had made history with her faded away.

Another of those early voters remained very much alive and continued to be condemned for joining the Anthony women in their crime. According to a story handed down by Rochester friends and neighbors, young Sarah Truesdale, who lived next door on the other side of the grape vine, was forbidden by her father to have anything to do with her famous neighbors after the arrests.

Susan seldom let other people's disapproval bother her. This incident, however, annoyed her greatly. That fall when the fruit ripened between their two yards, Susan picked every grape on her side of the fence. Mr. Truesdale no longer had enough to make his precious wine.

About two years after their arrest, the voting inspectors were thrown in jail for refusing to pay their fines. Going through with their prison sentence, Susan explained, would gain public sympathy for the cause of woman suffrage and might even get the men pardoned. If the inspectors were forgiven, then everyone would realize that Judge Hunt had conducted their trial in an unfair way.

Before leaving the jail, she promised the inspectors she would see that they were soon released. Although she had been willing to endure prison herself, she wrote in her journal that night, "I could not bear to come away and leave them one night in that dolorous place."

During the week the inspectors spent in jail, they received hundreds of visitors and enjoyed a continuous round of fine meals prepared by the women who had voted. After fighting for support for the inspectors, Susan was pleased to receive a telegram saying that President Grant had ordered their pardon. When the officials got out of jail, Susan's sister Hannah threw a big party for them and soon they returned to their old jobs as popular heroes.

How differently things turned out for Susan, who sacrificed far more than the inspectors! She never received a pardon, and her $100 fine stood against her for the rest of her life.

Both the trials and her nursing duties kept Susan away from earning money as a lecturer for a full year. Soon after burying Guelma, a Mr. Stillman said that he would sue her if she didn't pay him $500 for work he had done on the *Revolution*. Feeling heavy and slow with grief, she immediately took up her lecture tours again. "How like a millstone that *Revolution* debt hangs about my spirit," she wrote in her diary.

Although Mrs. Stanton had plenty of money, she again refused to help. The two women disagreed about many other issues, too. Still, whenever other suffragists wanted to remove Mrs. Stanton from office for saying outrageous things, Susan defended her old friend. And any time the two women appeared together at a convention, they always supported each other.

It took Susan six years of lecturing all over the country in order to pay off her newspaper debts. Susan, now a dignified 50-year-old woman, rode freight cars on trains at all hours of the day and night, endured 30-mile drives in mud and deep snow, and suffered through poor food and freezing hotel rooms. She took time off only for woman suffrage conventions and to nurse her brother Daniel, who was critically injured by a gunshot inflicted by a reader who disagreed with his newspaper.

Susan took an intense interest in her family. Daniel's wound threatened his life, the doctor warned. The only chance of keeping the patient alive was for someone to sit by him day and night and press on his artery to stop the bleeding. Even then, he would probably die.

Taking up this challenge, for nine weeks Susan took turns with other family members pressing on Daniel's artery. To everyone's amazement, he lived.

Susan bid Daniel goodbye and went back to her lecture tours. During these past difficult years, she had lost her right to elect the lawmakers of her country, labored under heavy debts, suffered illness and death in her family, and been let down by many of her friends. Still, her desire to win the vote for women burned strong.

Susan B. Anthony And Justice For All

Chapter Twelve: 1876-1890
Women Win with Words

Waiting in the broiling sun for the program to begin, men mopped their faces. Susan ignored the heat as best she could, for her petticoats and ruffles made her hot. But rather than complaining about the heat, she concentrated on pushing her way through the crowd in front of the speakers' platform.

It was July 1876, 100 years after the signing of the Declaration of Independence in Philadelphia. She and four friends were the only women allowed on stage during this anniversary party for the United States. With other fellow Americans, the suffragists had looked forward to this event that would announce to the world the progress their new country had made. The woman reformers had given $100,000 to help pay for the expenses of the lavish anniversary, hoping that American women would get noticed for accomplishments in business and service to their country. They were disappointed, therefore, when they learned that they would be mentioned only in the display of painting, sculpture, and other artwork.

The woman reformers appointed Susan as manager of their anniversary campaign and decided to set up their office close to the celebration. They promised to write a history of woman suffrage and send a copy to every woman who paid five dollars of the office expenses.

Next Mrs. Stanton and Matilda Joslyn Gage wrote the Woman's Declaration of 1876 and asked to present it at the anniversary celebration. Again they were refused, so they made plans of their own and waited for the chance to carry them out.

Gazing across the stage, Susan looked forward to the exact moment when she would give the signal to start their plan in motion. Silently, she thanked her brother Daniel for getting her permission to attend as a reporter for his paper. After a lot of pressure, the men in charge finally allowed her four woman friends to sit beside her. However, they had to sit in the back.

As the program began, Susan fanned herself while surveying the men in the seats of honor up front. Matilda leaned over and asked for the name of a certain man.

Susan said she thought it was Dom Pedro, emperor of Brazil.

Matilda frowned. Brazil! That country was about the farthest thing from democracy you could imagine. What was he doing at this celebration of liberty?

Susan fanned herself and sighed as she watched a 16-year-old prince of Sweden whisper something to Dom Pedro. Even the future king of a far-off nation enjoyed more honor than the women who had fought to make this country great.

Now someone was reading the Declaration of Independence from the original document signed in 1776. Susan listened with mixed feelings. It said such beautiful things about protecting the rights of the citizens of the United States. Too bad she had to create a fuss to remind people that women were citizens too.

Susan had a secret plan with the other women. They were going to be a part of the celebration after all. Her heart pounded as she consulted the program for the day's ceremonies. This was the moment.

"Now!" she said quietly, and signalled her friends to stand. While the Brazilian hymn played, they all processed down the aisle through the princes, kings, generals, and American statesmen who were standing around Vice-President Thomas Ferry, leader of the celebration.

"I present to you a Declaration of Rights from the women citizens of the United States," announced Susan in her clear voice.

Mr. Ferry turned to General Joseph Hawley, who had sent four passes to these women at the last minute. The vice-president's glance seemed to say, "I thought we agreed that this document was to have no part in today's proceedings." Hawley nodded but shrugged in defeat. Saying nothing to Susan, Ferry bowed and accepted the paper from her. Then to his relief, she and her friends moved as if to leave.

A moment later, however, Hawley hissed, "What are they doing now?" Ferry looked down to see the women handing out copies of the document as they went. Men were standing on their seats grabbing for the papers! The program interrupted, the band lapsed into silence while people craned their necks to watch the sea of sweating bodies part for the women.

At the United States' 100th birthday celebration in 1876,
Susan B. Anthony and friends handed out copies of the
Woman's Declaration of Independence.

"Order! Order!" Hawley cried as Susan reached the edge of the crowd.

Leaving the square, the women mounted a platform that had been set up for musicians near the Liberty Bell. Soon a bunch of curious people gathered. There, in front of Independence Hall, Susan reminded the audience that although women had worked to secure freedom for all citizens of every race in the United States, the women themselves would never be truly free until they could vote. The onlookers clapped and reached eagerly for copies of the Declaration.

Susan and her companions then proceeded to a suffrage meeting where Elizabeth Cady Stanton and many other friends congratulated them for their bold move. Reflecting on this day, they later wrote in the *History of Woman Suffrage,* "They determined to place on record for the women of 1976 the fact that their mothers of 1876 had asserted their equality of rights....Thus, in taking a grander step toward freedom than ever before, they would leave one bright remembrance for the women of the next Centennial."

For the rest of July the women kept their suffrage office open and enjoyed many visitors. By now Susan had put the *Revolution* debt behind her and Mrs. Stanton had announced that she was tired of lecture tours. Their common interests had held them together in spite of other disagreements. At the beginning of August, Matilda and the two old friends started writing the history of the woman's rights movement.

Susan planned to finish the several-hundred page booklet by December. After all, she had been keeping a diary and saved letters, reports, and news clippings for at least 25 years. She would sift through these materials and choose the best stories to include; the other two women would write it down.

The job of writing about the woman's movement proved much more difficult than she expected. After visiting several large publishers, she discovered that no one wanted to publish a book about such an unpopular topic. Accustomed to meeting financial challenges, she raised the necessary funds to pay for part of the printing. Later, she found a smaller company who agreed to publish the book. The three women who shared the work also agreed to divide the profits.

Because Susan wanted to give a truthful account of how women earned their rights, she asked many of the people active in the movement to send information about themselves. This, however, only added to her problems, for she found many of the handwritten replies almost impossible to read and full of mistakes. What was worse than the poor penmanship, however, was the note she received from woman's rights activist Lucy Stone, who said that she did not want any part of a book written by Susan and Mrs. Stanton. This hurt Susan deeply.

Lucy had been active in the woman's movement even longer than Susan. Like Susan and Mrs. Stanton, Lucy had endured all the teasing and mockery for wearing the bloomer. The three had campaigned together before the Civil War for abolition and woman's rights. After the war, however, Lucy had agreed with Frederick Douglass and others who said that Black men should vote before women.

Susan B. Anthony And Justice For All

Susan and Mrs. Stanton disagreed so strongly with this opinion that back in 1870 they had formed a separate organization called the National Woman Suffrage Association. They concentrated on pressuring Congress for a constitutional amendment so women could vote throughout all the states. Lucy founded the American Woman Suffrage Association, which tried to get individual states to allow women to vote.

Sometimes, when specific states like Kansas or California were deciding about woman suffrage, Susan and Mrs. Stanton gave lectures to help Lucy's organization. For the most part, however, the two groups remained rivals until 1890. They both worked for woman suffrage, but in different ways.

Lucy Stone was one of the people who criticized Mrs. Stanton and Susan sharply for using George Francis Train's money to start the *Revolution,* and shortly afterward started a rival paper called the *Woman's Journal.* Lucy refused to send Susan an account of her activities for the *History of Woman Suffrage* and later, when the book was published she, gave it a bad write-up in the *Woman's Journal.*

Writing felt like torture to Susan; several months into writing the *History of Woman Suffrage* she told a friend: "I am just sick to death of it. I had rather wash or whitewash or do any possible hard work than sit here and go there digging into the dusty records of the past — that is, rather make history than write it."

During the next ten years, Mrs. Stanton, Susan, and Matilda devoted every spare moment to writing down the history of the suffrage movement. Eventually they turned out four thick volumes.

Susan B. Anthony And Justice For All

In January 1877, Susan was relieved to put aside work on the book to go to Washington, where the National Association presented lawmakers with sack after sack of petitions for a woman suffrage amendment. The men were so unimpressed, that they paused just long enough to laugh as if the women had asked for something completely ridiculous. Then they went on with their other business.

In spite of such discouraging results, Susan pleaded for a woman suffrage amendment in Congress every year after that until she died in 1906. She knew that even when the lawmakers laughed, the discussion would still have to be recorded in the Congressional reports. Newspaper reporters, lawyers, and judges across the land would read and think about giving the vote to women. No matter how long it took, she would continue the fight.

In 1883, Susan (now 63) took several months off to visit Europe with Elizabeth Cady Stanton. Mrs. Stanton's daughter Harriot lived in England, and her home became the base from which the two now silver-haired women explored. During that trip Susan enjoyed famous historical sights and places of natural beauty, which she described in lively letters home. In one letter she begged "dear sister Mary" to shut up the house on Madison Street and join her for a few months.

Many of her writings from this journey, however, recounted her grief about the poverty that she saw in England and Ireland. In this letter to a friend, she showed that even when she was on holiday, her love for women was still tender enough that she would interrupt her sightseeing and go ten miles out of the way for a poor stranger:

"I saw...a ragged, bareheaded, barefooted woman tossing a wee baby over her shoulders and trying to get her apron switched around to hold it fast on her back....At that instant she succeeded in getting the baby adjusted, and to my horror took up a bundle from the grass and disclosed a second baby! Then I went down. I learned that she had just come from the poorhouse, where she had spent six weeks, and...she had heard that her old mother was ill in Milltown and had fretted about her till she could bear it no longer, so she had started to walk ten miles to her. I hailed a boy with a jaunting-car...and off we went, she sitting on one side of the car with her two babies, and I on the other."

During this trip, Susan met many women in England, France, and several other countries who were engaged in a similar battle for the woman's vote. She kept in touch with them and, five years later, hosted women from seven nations at the first International Congress on woman suffrage in the United States.

Besides giving Susan the satisfaction of working with people from all over the world for the same cause, the International Congress also marked the beginning of reunion with Lucy Stone and her organization. Supporters of woman's rights had often wondered why there were two organizations with similar names to accomplish the same goal. Now, at last, the two groups were forging a new friendship out of their past differences and jealousies.

Susan B. Anthony And Justice For All

The transition was far from smooth, however. One time, Antoinette Brown Blackwell (Lucy's sister-in-law) gave a long speech proving that she and Lucy had held meetings for woman suffrage a year before Elizabeth Cady Stanton or Susan B. Anthony had done anything for woman's rights. Somewhat grudgingly, Antoinette Blackwell wrote in a letter to Lucy Stone that Susan should eventually become president of the unified organization because as a spinster, she had given all of her time.

In 1890, they formed the National American Suffrage Association with Mrs. Stanton as president, Susan B. Anthony as vice-president, and Stone as head of an important committee. Gradually, both Mrs. Stanton and Lucy Stone experienced ill health and, as Blackwell predicted, Susan became president. Throughout her term of office she kept looking for opportunities to train younger women to take up the cause in her place.

Chapter Thirteen: 1891-1898

Passing the Torch

By 1891, Susan had spent 40 years traveling in all kinds of weather from one end of the continent to the other. Now 71 years old, she announced at the end of a long journey that she was going home to Rochester — to stay.

Well, most of the time, anyway. She firmly intended to leave the *hard* traveling to the many capable younger women she trained in her later years. Now she planned to direct the suffrage work from behind the scenes, writing hundreds of letters each month in her comfortably furnished study on the second floor. Also, there were more books on the woman's movement to publish (with the help of a capable writer, of course) and she wanted them to be written in the comfort of her own home.

Of course, she still had little trips planned to neighboring towns; and she would never miss an annual suffrage convention, which was usually held in Washington, D.C. Even so, these outings away from Rochester were spaced far enough apart that she had time to enjoy her home, so beautifully redecorated and refurnished by loving friends. They even held a reception for 300 people to celebrate Susan's "coming home" in 1891. Flowers scented every room for the occasion. New easy chairs and new drapes brightened up the parlor, where the spinning wheel that Mother had received as a bridal gift stood before the handsome fireplace.

The old house held many memories of Guelma and her children, Hannah, and Mother, who had all died. Having weathered these wrenching family losses, Susan treasured her companionship with her youngest sister Mary all the more now.

In spite of her many griefs (or perhaps to distract herself from them), Susan pushed on with her work. She had rejoiced in 1890 when the new state of Wyoming joined the United States; their women had been voting since 1869 and continued to do so in state elections. There was still much work to do, however, because women from Wyoming could not vote in national elections.

Now that Mrs. Stanton had become a widow and her children were grown, Susan looked forward to a closer relationship with her best friend. "Come live with me on Madison Street," she wrote Mrs. Stanton, who had sold her home in New Jersey. Mrs. Stanton, however, chose to move in with two of her married children in New York, maintaining the separation that Susan longed to overcome.

But the two friends continued to cook up schemes in order to gain new rights for women. In 1891, during Mrs. Stanton's month-long visit to Susan's "new" home, they began trying to get women admitted into Rochester's university. They launched their effort with a reception for 200 at Madison Street. The board

Susan B. Anthony and Elizabeth Cady Stanton remained
close friends for more than 50 years.
University of Rochester

of trustees who made the important decisions at the university gave many reasons why women should not attend. First, they said the presence of females would distract the male students from their studies. Second, they suggested that a separate school be opened for women. No, replied Susan, thinking of her experience as a student of Miss Moulson, she wanted women to have the same educational opportunities as men.

She continued her efforts to have women officially welcomed at the university. She quietly paid the tuition for Helen Eveline Wilkinson to attend college. However, this was only a partial victory: although the young woman could go to lectures and take notes, she was not allowed to speak in class and none of her work was graded.

Next, the trustees said that women could attend as full-fledged students if they gave the university $100,000 to add facilities. Although this seemed a ridiculously large sum, female reformers agreed to raise the money and were given several years to do so. Busy with suffrage activities, Susan left most of this fundraising effort to other women she knew and trusted.

Meanwhile, Susan was becoming impatient to publish a record of her personal life. For several months she searched for a competent writer who would help her sift through her memories and do the writing. She finally found that person in Ida Husted Harper, who had been a successful newspaper writer.

In 1897, Ida moved into the Anthony household to help Susan write her life story. Susan assured the author that it wouldn't take long to write because she had all the information at her fingertips.

After Mary Anthony helped Ida settle in her room, Susan opened the door to the attic and turned on the light. Grasping the wooden handrail, she told the writer that she'd find everything she needed up there. For example, Susan had about 20,000 letters, some dating back to her parents' time.

"It sounds like a researcher's dream," replied the writer. She couldn't wait to start.

Mary hoped the papers were worth saving, because she had been trying to get her sister to throw some of that old junk away for years.

Susan climbed the stairs slowly, for they were steep and dark. Mary followed behind Ida. When Susan reached the top, she paused for breath and pointed with a sweeping gesture around the room. Ida's eyes followed, and then she gasped.

Yes, everything she needed was certainly here — but how would she ever find it? Boxes and bags of letters, some from 1797, were tied in bundles. Sixty years of Susan's diaries were jumbled up with receipts, records of expenses, and speeches. At first, the Anthonys had been really good about pasting things into scrapbooks, but after awhile the material piled up so fast that no one could keep up with the job.

"On the wall are the records from every year that Mrs. Stanton and I have spoken before Congress," Susan said proudly. "You'll find many of Mrs. Stanton's fine speeches in there."

The author carefully removed a pile of old magazines from a chair and sat down with a sigh. This would make a wonderful book, but how long would it take to sort through this mess before she could begin?

Ida Harper set several stenographers, or secretaries, to work on sorting and organizing the papers. Soon everything was lined up in neat boxes all around the attic workroom. The author made Susan promise that she would stay home until the writing was done. Susan gave her word to remain nearby, but soon found herself taking one "short trip" after another, leaving Ida alone to work on the biography. Eventually, *The Life and Work of Susan B. Anthony* grew into three huge volumes; the writer completed the final book after Susan's death.

Despite her advancing age, Susan kept working hard for the woman's movement. Even now, she continued her lifelong habit of rising at seven o'clock every morning and starting with a cold bath. From the cluttered desk in her second-floor study, she wrote hundreds of letters every month to old friends and to younger women whom she had prepared to continue the task of getting the vote for woman.

Many letters flew back and forth between Susan and Anna Howard Shaw, the most powerful orator for the woman's cause. Susan felt deeply stirred by the stately minister's preaching at the International Congress and many other places. Anna's vision of the woman suffrage movement was so similar that Susan allowed the younger woman to call her "Aunt Susan." It was important for Susan to keep in touch with followers like Shaw who would carry woman's reform into the twentieth century.

Several stenographers helped Susan work more quickly by typing her letters and speeches. Susan must have kept them plenty busy because one of them, who admired her famous employer very much, confessed that Susan made her work harder than anyone else ever had.

Another stenographer disobeyed Susan's orders and got fired. Susan had invited a Black speaker named Ida Wells to stay at Madison Street and told her guest that she could make use of Susan's stenographer Anna to type her letters. When Susan came back later in the day, however, she saw Ida Wells still struggling to handwrite everything.

"Couldn't you dictate, and let Anna type for you?" she asked. The Black woman kept silent.

Then Susan understood, and marched upstairs to ask Anna why she hadn't helped the minister.

"I didn't choose to write for a colored woman, I engaged to work for you," she replied.

"When I ask an employee to do a favor for a guest, I expect her to comply," Susan shot back.

"It's all right for you to treat Negroes as equals, but I refuse to take dictation from a colored woman," the young woman said stubbornly.

"If that is the way you feel about it, you needn't stay any more," Susan replied. Nudging Anna, she said none too gently, "Come, get your bonnet and go."

For her 80th birthday in 1900, Susan B. Anthony received
80 roses from children.
Museum of American History

Chapter Fourteen: 1898
The Costly Campaign in Rochester

Busy with writing the biography and with voting issues across the country, Susan had not kept a very watchful eye on the group that was raising funds to get women admitted to the university in Rochester. The fund-raisers had worked so hard that the school agreed to settle for only $50,000 instead of the $100,000 required at the beginning. But in September of 1898, time was running out. Susan returned from a trip to learn that only one day was left until the entire amount was due, and the women had raised only $42,000.

Now an old woman, Susan sadly admitted that she had lost some of the energy she had enjoyed when she was younger. Still travel-weary from her long journey, she began making her pleas for money early in the morning on an Indian summer day. Over the years her sister Mary had saved $2,000 to give young women once they were admitted to the school.

"Give it now or they won't get in at all," Susan urged, and Mary did.

Next, Susan hired an open carriage and went bumping along over brick and cobblestone streets asking for contributions from people she knew. It jolted her old bones painfully, but she felt she had to make this last effort for the young women of her city.

Like Mary, the minister and his wife at the Unitarian Church also contributed $2,000, as did her old friend Sarah L. Willis.

But now, noted Susan glancing at her watch, it was past noon. Only a few hours remained, and she still needed the remaining $2,000. Desperately, she searched her memory for somewhere else to turn.

Finally, as the trustees opened their meeting, Susan secured a promise for the money from Samuel Wilder, a well-known elder Rochester man. Hot and more tired than ever, she rushed into the meeting.

In a voice shaking with excitement, she announced, "I've met the goal."

Was she expecting the men to rejoice with her? If so, she was sorely disappointed. Instead, they avoided her eyes while they shuffled papers, closely examining every name and dollar pledged. When they reached Wilder's contribution, they frowned and shook their heads. He was too old, they objected; he might die before he ever gave the money to the university.

Susan could stand no more delay. Drawing herself up to her full height, she replied in a firm voice that she would pay the money with her own life insurance policy. "I asked Mr. Wilder to lend me his name so that this question of co-education might not be hurt by any connection with woman suffrage." Despite her promise, the university officials told her to come back while they debated their answer for a few more days.

The next evening, she wrote with a shaky hand in her diary, "Went to church today but had a sleepy time

— such a sleepy time. It seemed as if something was the matter with my tongue — I had a feeling of strangeness — could not think what I wanted to say....Mary asked me several times if anything was the matter."

The next morning she did not speak at all. Summoning all her strength, she went to the university to learn of their decision. As soon as she returned home from this meeting, she wrote with a wavering line in her diary, "They let the girls in. He said there was no alternative."

This victory for the women of her city gave Susan little joy. In her diary she wrote, "Not a trustee has given anything although there are several millionaires among them." Also, she was feeling even more weak and tired. On the evening the trustees said yes to women, a crowd gathered at the Anthony home to celebrate. She sat in her usual chair and tried to smile, but her face looked white. She disappeared up the stairs. Mary found her unconscious on the bed; Susan had suffered a stroke.

The doctor visited and checked on her for a whole month. For the first week Susan could hardly speak, but gradually she regained the ability to do so. When she felt well enough to leave the house, she asked to be taken for a carriage ride through the university. "As I drove over the campus, I felt 'these are not forbidden grounds to the girls of the city any longer.' It is good to feel that the old doors sway on their hinges — to women!"

Unfortunately, Susan never did regain her strength. The doctor predicted that she probably never would and warned that she might have another stroke any time. She should stay warm and avoid crowds, he warned. Susan, however, decided it was better to take risks with her health than sit around doing nothing, so the next month she went to a huge gathering in New York City — out in the cold. She survived that trip and several others, but the effort to travel was costing her more and more.

Chapter Fifteen: 1901-1906
One Step Higher

By 1901 Susan had the satisfaction of knowing that women were allowed to vote in three more western states — Colorado, Utah, and Idaho. Rejoicing in these victories, she still desperately wanted a federal amendment that would allow every American woman in every state to vote for all elected officials, including president and vice-president. As her 80th birthday approached that year, she turned over the presidency of the suffrage association to the capable hands of Carrie Chapman Catt.

Even without the presidency, Susan still found plenty to do. With Lucy Stone, Elizabeth Cady Stanton, and others, she had launched the movement toward woman suffrage more than half a century earlier. Now she gave most of her time to making sure that younger women were ready to take over the responsibility when the old-timers were gone. Busy as she was preparing for the future, Susan still took time to stay in touch with her old friend Mrs. Stanton.

During their long friendship, they had disagreed many times. In the early years when the married woman drew more applause with her charming stories of family life, Susan had envied Mrs. Stanton's popularity. Later, when Mrs. Stanton was writing books about religion that angered many suffragists, she longed for the praise that Susan enjoyed from reformers all over the country. Through it all, however, the two remained friends.

At a birthday celebration for Susan, Mrs. Stanton said, "Nothing gives me more intense satisfaction than my friendship...with Susan B. Anthony. Ours has been a friendship of hard work and self-denial." Then she went on in a joking manner, "Emerson says, 'It is better to be a thorn in the side of your friend than his echo.' If this add weight and stability to friendship, then ours will endure forever, for we have indeed been thorns in the side of each other."

Although she was now 82 and had suffered a stroke, Susan enjoyed better health than Mrs. Stanton, who had become blind and seriously overweight. Susan journeyed to see her friend twice in 1902, and prepared a special celebration for Mrs. Stanton's 87th birthday.

Who can imagine, then, Susan's grief when she received the news that Mrs. Stanton died two weeks before her birthday party? Stunned and silent, trying to absorb the awful truth, Susan sat alone in her study for hours. Finally, as twilight deepened into darkness, reporters came and pressed her for comments about her famous friend.

"For 50 years there has been an unbroken friendship between us," she said. "We did not agree on every point, but on the central point of woman suffrage we always agreed....I cannot express myself at all as I feel, I am too crushed to speak. If I had died first she would have found beautiful phrases to describe our friendship, but I cannot put it into words. She always said she wanted to outlive me so that she could give her tribute to the world."

It was Susan who sat beside Mrs. Stanton's casket. On the day of the funeral she said, "Oh, this awful hush! It seems impossible that voice is stilled which I have loved to hear for 50 years. Always I have felt that I must have Mrs. Stanton's opinion of things before I knew where I stood myself....What a world it is, it goes on and on just the same no matter who lives or who dies!"

In the remaining years of her life, almost every month brought news of the death of another of Susan's old friends. In addition, for the last four years of her life, she suffered great weakness, serious bouts of pneumonia, and frightening episodes with her heart.

As she wrote in her diary, "It sometimes acts as if I had been running at the top of my speed, and then it almost stops....I hear its beating, awake or asleep." Hardly anyone besides her sister Mary knew of her discomforts, for she kept them to herself and did what she could. She often felt frustrated that she could not do as much speaking, traveling, and writing as she wanted to.

The year before her death, when asked to lecture, she replied that nothing would give her more joy, but "I am done with making speeches for any purpose whatsoever," and then she recommended one of the many younger women that she had trained to take her place.

In February 1906, friends persuaded her to attend

a celebration of her 86th birthday in Baltimore. There she gathered what little energy she had to thank the many women of the National Association who were carrying on the work she loved so well. Realizing that her strength was almost gone, she finished, "There have been many others also just as true and devoted to the cause...but with such women consecrating their lives, failure is impossible!"

The following month she caught pneumonia, and her health grew rapidly worse. As Susan lay dying in the little back bedroom on Madison Street, Anna Howard Shaw and Mary Anthony took turns holding her hand. During her last hours, Susan saw behind her closed eyes a parade of the many strong women and men who had labored at her side for so many years, and greeted each one. In the early hours of the morning, she slipped away.

The day of her funeral, 10,000 people waited patiently in the heavily falling snow to take one last look at Susan's face before she was buried. As the leader of many movements and the president of many councils, Susan had achieved world fame. On that day, however, mourners were less concerned with her public side than with the generous woman they had known. Many told personal stories of "Aunt Susan," who shared their joys and griefs, fought private battles for close friends, and welcomed them into her Madison Street home.

Mrs. Jeffrey, a dignified Black woman, said at the funeral, "We, the colored people of Rochester, join the world in mourning the loss of our true friend, Susan B. Anthony....She was our great friend for many years

— our champion. Sleep on, dear heart, in peace, for we who have looked into thy face, we who have heard thy voice, we who have known something of thy great life work — we pledge ourselves to devote our time and energies to the work thou has left us to do."

Anna Howard Shaw gave the final address, saying, "Her work will not be finished, nor will her last word be spoken, while there remains a wrong to be righted or a fettered life to be freed in all the earth."

Susan B. Anthony's strength and inspiration carried her 20th-century followers over bridges that Susan herself had never crossed. Fourteen more years passed before her vision of voting rights for American women become a reality. Finally in 1920, Congress passed the Nineteenth Amendment giving women throughout the United States the right to vote. Susan's dearest wish came true. Often called the Susan B. Anthony Amendment, it is the most fitting reminder of the woman who gave her life so that others might enjoy the rights and responsibilities of full citizens.

Many years after Susan's death, people from all over the world still visit her hometown of Rochester, New York to gather strength from her powerful and victorious struggle. As they join the stream of women and men students changing classes at the Rochester university, visitors might catch a glimpse of the dormitory named after Susan B. Anthony. Climbing the hilly, wooded paths near Susan's grave in Mount Hope Cemetery, they might reflect that life hasn't changed all that much since her time. Although some battles have already been won, many women and

Susan B. Anthony And Justice For All

African-Americans continue to struggle for rights that others take for granted. Susan would agree that much remains to be done.

Still more people make the trip to see Susan's red brick home on Madison Street. They examine the photographs and paintings of people she respected and worked with in three reform movements — temperance, woman suffrage, and abolition. Standing in the front parlor, they listen to stories about Marshal Keeney's refusal to handcuff the lady who broke the law by voting. They admire the easy chair given to her by some of the first woman graduates of the University of Rochester. And holding onto the bannister of the old staircase, they feel Susan's strength carry them one step higher toward a vision of the day when there is justice for all.

§§§

Glossary

Abolition: The movement to end slavery in the United States.

Activist: A person who works to cause a political change or transition in society.

Amendment: A revision or change made to the Constitution.

Antislavery: The belief that slavery is wrong.

Auction: A public market where goods are sold for money.

Bail: Money paid to release prisoners from jail, guaranteeing their return for trial.

Ballot: The piece of paper on which men and women write their choice of candidates when they vote.

Bloomer: An outfit worn by women during the 1850s. It consisted of trousers that gather at the ankle underneath a skirt cropped at the knee.

Campaign: An organized effort to bring about a change in society.

Co-education: The education of boys and girls together.

Constitution: The document that states the laws of the United States.

Convention: A meeting where people discuss a specific issue in order to reach an agreement.

Debt: Money owed to a person or organization.

Deed: A written letter or agreement that acts as proof of ownership.

District Attorney: The lawyer who tries to prove that a prisoner is guilty of a crime.

Dolorous: Sad and gloomy.

Equality: Having the same value as another person or thing.

Inheritance: Goods or money received from a relative at his or her death.

Judgment: An opinion; usually made by someone of authority such as a judge.

Jury: A group of citizens who hears all the evidence in a legal trial and decides whether the person is guilty or innocent.

Liberation: The act or process of being freed in order to achieve equal rights.

Mills: A factory where cotton is made into cloth.

Movement: The actions of a group of people working towards a certain goal for political change.

Overseer: A boss or supervisor who watches the workers in order to make sure that the job gets done correctly.

Petition: A document signed by a number of people asking for change.

Petticoats: Undergarments that a woman wears beneath her skirt.

Pioneers: The first or earliest group to explore or settle new land; the first people to do something.

Plantation: A farm, usually in the South, where crops are raised.

Quaker: A religious group (also called the Society of Friends) who believe in hard work and peaceful living.

Reformer: One whose actions try to make a political change.

Slave: A person who has lost all rights of freedom and is forced to work for a master without pay.

Spinster: An unmarried woman who is considered too old to be single.

Stenographer: A person who writes letters in short-hand; a secretary.

Suffragist: A person who supports the right for all people to vote.

Supreme Court: The highest court in the United States.

Temperance: Movement to stop people from making and drinking alcoholic beverages.

Trustee: A person who is in charge of making decisions for a college or other institution.

United States Congress: A group of people who discuss political problems.

Underground Railroad: A system of safe places set up by abolitionists to help escaped slaves as they traveled from the South to freedom in Canada.

Wages: The payment of money for work.

Warrant: A document giving an officer the right to arrest a person.

Important Events in the Life of Susan B. Anthony

February 15, 1820	Susan Brownell Anthony born near Adams, Massachusetts
1824	Susan learns to read from her grandmother
1826	Family moves to Battenville, New York; Father starts a school
1838	Father goes bankrupt and must sell family belongings at an auction. Family moves to Hardscrabble, New York
1845	The Anthonys move to a farm in Rochester, New York
1846	Susan becomes headmistress of the Female Department at Canajoharie Academy, upstate New York
1848	First Woman's Rights Convention held by Elizabeth Cady Stanton in Seneca Falls
1849	Susan gives her first public speech; joins Daughters of Temperance

1851	Susan meets Elizabeth Cady Stanton
1852	Susan founds New York Women's State Temperance Society; attends first woman's rights convention
1853-54	Susan wears bloomers
1853-60	Susan campaigns in New York regarding women's property rights and suffrage
1854-55	Susan visits 54 counties in New York State in four months for married women's rights
1856	Susan becomes principal New York agent for Garrison's American Anti-Slavery Society
1860	Married Women's Property Act passes
1861-1865	The Civil War
1864	Women's National Loyal League sends Congress 400,000 petitions against slavery
1865	Thirteenth Amendment outlaws the slavery of African-Americans
1866	Lucy, Susan, and Mary Anthony move to Madison Street. Susan campaigns for inclusion of woman suffrage guarantee in Fourteenth Amendment

1868	Fourteenth Amendment makes Black men citizens and gives them rights
1870	Fifteenth Amendment gives Black men the right to vote; right to vote shall not be denied on account of race, color, or previous condition of servitude
1868-1870	Susan publishes The *Revolution*
1872	Susan is arrested for voting illegally
1873	Guelma dies of tuberculosis
1890	At the age of 71, Susan sets up housekeeping with Mary. Wyoming is the first state to grant woman suffrage
1896	Idaho and Utah get the vote for women
1897	Susan starts her biography
1898	Susan persuades Rochester university to admit women
1902	Elizabeth Cady Stanton dies
1906	Susan attends her last woman suffrage convention
March 13, 1906	Susan dies
1920	Nineteenth Amendment gives all women in the United States the right to vote

Selections
for Young Readers

Beale, Irene A. *Genesee Valley Women 1743-1985.* Geneseo, New York: Chestnut Hill Press, 1985.

Cox, Clinton. *Undying Glory: The Story of the Massachusetts 54th Regiment.* New York: Scholastic Inc., Book-Stratford Press, 1963.

Cullen-Dupont, Kathryn. *Elizabeth Cady Stanton and Women's Liberty.* New York: Facts On File, 1992.

Jacobs, William Jay. *Mother, Aunt Susan and Me: The First Fight For Women's Rights.* New York: Coward, McCann and Geoghegan, 1979.

McMullan, Kate. *Harriet Tubman, Conductor of The Underground Railroad.* New York: Parachute Press, 1991.

Morrison, Dorothy Nafus. *Ladies Were Not Expected: Abigail Scott Duniway and Women's Rights.* New York: Atheneum, 1977.

Weiner, Eric. *The Story of Frederick Douglass, Voice of Freedom.* Parachute Press, Inc., 1992.

Weisberg, Barbara. *Susan B. Anthony, Woman Suffragist.* New York: Chelsea House, 1988.

Further Reading

Barry, Kathleen. *Susan B. Anthony: Biography of a Singular Feminist.* New York University Press, 1988.

Duster, Alfreda M., ed. *Crusade for Justice: The Autobiography of Ida B. Wells.* Chicago: University of Chicago Press, 1970.

Griffith, Elizabeth. *In Her Own Right: The Life of Elizabeth Cady Stanton.* New York: Oxford University Press, 1984

Harper, Ida Husted. *The Life and Work of Susan B. Anthony.* 3 volumes. Indianapolis: Bowen-Merrill Co., 1899-1908.

Lasser, Carol and Merrill, Marlene Deahl, eds. *Friends and Sisters: Lucy Stone and Antoinette Brown Blackwell.* Chicago: University of Illinois Press, 1987.

Lutz, Alma. *Susan B. Anthony: Rebel, Crusader, Humanitarian.* Boston: Beacon, 1959.

Merrill, Arch. *The Underground, Freedom's Road and Other Upstate Tales.* New York: American Book-Stratford Press, 1963.

Scrapbook of Helen Eveline Wilkinson. Department of Rare Books and Special Collections, University of Rochester Library

About This Book

While working as an education and history reporter in Rochester, New York, Jeanne Gehret toured Susan B. Anthony's home and gravesite in 1988. Soon after, she started writing a series of books and tucked away the information about the famous woman for future use.

Four years later, while resting up from the publication of her third book, the author began volunteering as a tour guide at Susan's house.

Now she was hungry to learn all she could about Miss Anthony's life and times. She found herself delving into the dress and customs of the 19th century, reading about its reformers, and visiting many of Susan's favorite locations in Rochester, Washington, and Seneca Falls. The research and writing of this book have been gladdened by the friendship of professionals and volunteers who keep the memory of Susan B. Anthony alive today.

§§§

Index